S0-AEB-739

CHINA AND AMERICA

COUNCIL ON FOREIGN RELATIONS BOOKS

The Council on Foreign Relations, Inc. is a non-profit and non-partisan organization devoted to promoting improved understanding of international affairs through the free exchange of ideas. Its membership of about 1,700 persons throughout the United States is made up of individuals with special interest and experience in international affairs. The Council has no affiliation with, and receives no funding from, the United States government. The Council does not take any position on questions of foreign policy.

The Council publishes the quarterly journal, *Foreign Affairs*. In addition, from time to time, books and monographs written by members of the Council's research staff or visiting fellows, or commissioned by the Council, or (like this book) written by independent authors with critical review contributed by a Council study group, are published with the designation "Council on Foreign Relations Book" or "Council Paper on International Affairs." Any book or monograph bearing that designation is, in the judgment of the Committee on Studies of the Council's board of directors, a responsible treatment of a significant international topic worthy of presentation to the public. All statements of fact and expressions of opinion contained in Council books, monographs, and *Foreign Affairs* articles are, however, the sole responsibility of their authors.

CHINA AND AMERICA

The Search for a New

Relationship

Edited by
WILLIAM J. BARNDS

A Council on Foreign Relations Book
Published by
New York University Press · New York · 1977

Copyright 1977 by Council on Foreign Relations, Inc.
Library of Congress Catalog Card Number: 76-46694
ISBN: 0-8147-0989-3

Library of Congress Cataloging in Publication Data

Main entry under title:

China and America.

   "A Council on Foreign Relations book."
   Includes bibliographical references and index.
   1. United States—Relations (general) with China—
Addresses, essays, lectures. 2. China—Relations
(general) with the United States—Addresses, essays,
lectures. I. Barnds, William J. II. Council on
Foreign Relations.
E183.8.C5C445   301.29'73'051   76-46694
ISBN 0-8147-0989-3

Manufactured in the United States of America

In memoriam
ALEXANDER ECKSTEIN
1915-1976

Contents

Preface

This book grew out of a series of discussions held at the Council on Foreign Relations during 1975-76 on the evolution of Sino-American relations (especially since the early 1970s) and on the issues and considerations that would determine the future course of the relationship. The discussions were prompted by an awareness that after a few years of steady movement toward establishing a new and more constructive relationship progress had slowed dramatically if not ground to a halt. The shared concern over Soviet power that led Chinese and American leaders to a normalization of Sino-American relations remained. But diminished Chinese fears of a Soviet attack and growing Chinese concern over the United States' pursuit of a policy of détente with the Soviet Union were creating new uncertainties about the value of the relationship. Political disarray in both China and the United States also limited the ability of the two governments to move ahead, and the Taiwan issue was proving intractable in these circumstances.

Several specialists on Chinese affairs were asked to prepare papers to aid the group assess the implications of recent developments and to address the key issues that were likely to determine the future course of Sino-American relations. They were also asked to set forth their own ideas regarding the appropriate policies for the United States to follow in dealing with China, one of the key nations in the world.

Professor Akira Iriye of the University of Chicago appraises the evolving Chinese perceptions of the international system and the role policy toward the United States has played in Chinese foreign policy over the past thirty years, and the issues facing the new Chinese leadership today. Professor Alexander Eckstein of the University of Michigan analyzed the shifting role of foreign trade in Chinese economic strategy, the evolution of Sino-American economic relations since 1970, and the prospects for and constraints upon such relations in the future. Professor Lucian Pye of the Massachusetts Institute of Technology appraises both the official and the unofficial cultural exchange programs that have developed since 1971 against the background of the underlying cultural traits of the two societies, and weighs the advantages and disadvantages of various courses of action open to the U.S. government to ensure that such exchanges contribute to a sounder relationship. Ralph Clough of The Brookings Institution discusses the role of the Republic of China on Taiwan, both as a country in its own right and in terms of its importance in Sino-American relations, and concludes with recommendations for U.S. policy in this difficult matter. In the final chapter, I analyze the key issues involved in American policy toward China, and suggest guidelines for U.S. policy toward China in relation to our over-all policies in Asia, especially those dealing with the Soviet Union and Japan.

The group which met at the Council was chaired by James

[x]

F. Leonard, and included A. Doak Barnett, Thomas P. Bernstein, Paul Borsuk, William P. Bundy, Ralph N. Clough, Col. Arthur E. Dewey, Alexander Eckstein, Leslie H. Gelb, William H. Gleysteen, Selig S. Harrison, Akira Iriye, Jan H. Kalicki, Edward Klein, Steven I. Levine, Kenneth Lieberthal, James Lilley, Winston Lord, Abraham F. Lowenthal, Kenneth P. Morse, Michel Oksenberg, Michael J. O'Neill, Christopher H. Phillips, Lucian W. Pye, Arthur Rosen, Warner R. Schilling, R. Grant Smith, Richard H. Solomon, Walter Sterling Surrey, Francis R. Valeo, and Donald S. Zagoria.

We were also fortunate to have T.D. Allman, William Diebold, Jr., Robert Michael Field, Anne Keatley, and Richard Ullman present at individual meetings. All the authors benefited from these discussions and wish to thank the members of the group for many helpful suggestions. The views expressed in the book, of course, are the authors' own.

I wish to express my appreciation to James F. Leonard for his excellent work as chairman of the group and to Michael Baron for his work as rapporteur. Abraham F. Lowenthal, Director of Studies while this volume was under preparation, provided continued counsel and encouragement, as did my colleagues on the Council's Studies Staff. Robert Valkenier's assistance went far beyond that of simply editing the individual papers, and all the authors express their appreciation to him. Thanks are also due to Donald Wasson, Janet Rigney, and other members of the library staff for their assistance in locating books and documents, and to Lorna Brennan and her staff for arranging the meetings. I am particularly indebted to my research associate, Helen Caruso, in providing valuable assistance on many of the topics analyzed in this book, and to my secretary Zenaida Zapanta for her assistance with the manuscript. And I wish to thank Professor Robert F. Dernberger of the University of Michigan for updating certain figures and reading the proofs of Chapter 3.

It is unfortunately necessary to conclude on a sad note. Professor Alexander Eckstein died of a heart attack in December 1976 shortly after having completed the final revisions of his chapter. Alex's contribution to the field of Chinese studies is far too well known to require any description here. He was a prodigious worker, and had made important contributions to our knowledge of Chinese economic policy. Among his many works was *Communist China's Economic Growth and Foreign Trade* (1966), which he had written for the Council. He had also contributed articles to *Foreign Affairs.* All who work in the area of Chinese studies, and all of us at the Council on Foreign Relations, are in his debt and are the poorer for his death.

April 1977 W.J.B.

[ONE]

Introduction

William J. Barnds

The attempt of the United States and China to work out a new and less hostile relationship has proved to be a slow and arduous task. From 1971 until late 1973 or 1974, as progress was made, many Americans tended to assume that a new era had dawned and to confuse the easing of Sino-American hostility with the forging of a cooperative relationship, which is a much more long-range and uncertain endeavor. As a result of the slackened momentum since 1974 and the new leaders in office in both countries, the two governments are re-examining the developments of the past few years and reappraising the benefits and costs, actual and potential, of the relationship before making any new moves. The pendulum may not have swung back toward hostility in the United States, but there is an air of skepticism.

To emphasize the difficulties in establishing a better Sino-American relationship should not lead us to underrate the dramatic effects of the steps already taken. The opening to China, taken against the backdrop of the Sino-Soviet dispute, has had a profound effect on the international scene. The

Soviet Union has found that many of its gains around the world—its acknowledged strategic parity with the United States, Western recognition of the status quo in Europe, and a growing Soviet naval force which is providing it with a global reach—have been offset by the costs of its bitter quarrel with China. The clear-cut lines of the Cold War have become blurred, but by differing degrees in different parts of Asia; e.g., in Thailand, compared to the Korean peninsula. The Sino-Soviet dispute has benefited Japan, providing it with an opportunity to expand its relations with its giant neighbors without alienating the United States. The dispute has been costly to China militarily and economically, but the shift in Chinese foreign policy since 1970 has enabled it to neutralize one of its major adversaries (the United States), obtain diplomatic recognition from many countries, and gain a greatly enhanced status in the world and in international organizations. Finally, the opening to China provided an opportunity for a weary and divided America to offset its weaknesses of spirit by taking advantage of the bitter enmity between Moscow and Peking.

The changes which have occurred have been dramatic, yet there are two further points to note. The first is the length of time it took for these changes to develop. It was more than *ten* years after the eruption of the Sino-Soviet dispute before China and the United States began to move toward a rapprochment. There are explanations for this slow pace: the legacy of hostility exacerbated by the Korean War, sharply contrasting ideological outlooks, the impact of the Vietnam War, and China's turning inward during the Great Cultural Revolution. These events all created constraints on working out a new relationship. But over *five* years after the break-through in the early 1970s, the leaders of the two countries can say no more than that they remain determined to normalize relations—at some unspecified date. The achievements of recent years should not be underrated, and stalemates or even setbacks should not surprise us after steady progress between 1971 and 1974. Explanations are again possible: the intractability of the Taiwan issue, the impact of the sudden collapse in Vietnam, domestic political problems in both countries, and the desire of each government to obtain the best possible terms in any bargain that is struck.

Nor should we overlook a second element, namely, that the changes of the past five years may have been more dramatic than they have been basic or possibly even durable. One hopes that this is not the case. However, anyone familiar with the history of Sino-American relations, the complexity of the foreign policy goals of each country, and the impact of domestic politics on their foreign policies can find numerous reasons for keeping expectations modest. Both countries have had a strong sense of the superiority of their own culture. The Chinese view of their country as the Middle Kingdom, hardly unreasonable given their unique historical record and achievements, was matched by the American view of their own society as unique—as "a chosen country" or as "the last, best hope on earth." At the same time, the United States—in contrast to China—had a missionary outlook (in the broadest sense of the term). As Stanley Karnow commented a few years ago on shifting American views of China:

> In large measure, I think, both the media and the public have swung from extreme hostility to extreme affection—and could swing back again—because they share a peculiarly American passion about China. That feeling has been described as a "love-hate" syndrome, but I would describe it as a sense of responsibility toward China. While other Western nations have accepted the

Chinese as they were, we tried to befriend them and mold them into our own shape.[1]

If most outsiders now realize the limitations on their power to influence the course of events in China, few Chinese have forgotten that their country experienced a century of weakness, disruption, and humiliation at the hands first of the West and then of the Japanese. China was never reduced to the status of a colony, but many of its tributary states were detached and foreign nations carved out spheres of influence inside China itself. China thus went from dominance to inferiority without experiencing life in an international society composed of independent states of equal status and roughly equal power.

In short, the relationship between China and the West, including the United States, has been basically asymmetrical. While the extent of the asymmetry has been reduced since the Communists established a strong central government in China, it has not been eliminated. A central question for the Chinese for over a century has been how to respond to the impact of the West. Despite the vastly different position of the China of 1975 from the China of 1900 or 1925, the issue remains an important one in Chinese politics.[2]

If the Chinese—in contrast to the Japanese—have been uncertain and divided over the appropriate response to the Western intrusion, there have also been sharp fluctuations in American views of China and the appropriate policy toward that country that have undoubtedly been puzzling to the Chinese. These fluctuations need not be elaborated here. It is useful to remember, however, that the antagonism between China and the United States—growing out of contrasting values and ideologies, the U.S. involvement with the Chinese Nationalists, Peking's alliance with Moscow, and the Sino-

American war in Korea—set the tone of Sino-American relations that dominated much of Asian affairs for two decades. The residue of that hostility among the leaders and peoples of both countries, and its effect on East Asian politics generally, remains a burden to those who are now attempting to work out a better relationship between two countries which have never had a good relationship when both were strong.

The problem is also complicated by the dilemmas facing both countries. The United States wants China to be strong enough to serve as a check on Soviet power, and has tried to utilize the Sino-Soviet dispute to improve Sino-American relations. At the same time, American leaders have tried to reassure China's smaller neighbors, some of whom are U.S. allies, that we are still opposed to Chinese hegemony in Asia. Such ambiguity is not easy for the United States to handle in view of its history, diversity, and structure of government. The corresponding Chinese dilemma was concisely stated by a British observer in 1975:

> Were the United States to withdraw from South Korea, Taiwan, and perhaps elsewhere in East Asia following her recent defeats, both the durability and indeed the military value of remaining American commitments would be highly doubtful. The dilemma to China therefore is to what extent she can oppose specific important outposts of the American military deployment in East Asia, without undermining American credibility as a countervailing power in the area . . .[3]

The impact of domestic politics in each country on its policy toward the other remains as perplexing as it is important. How well do the leaders and officials of each government understand the other? (How many Americans foresaw the rise of Hua Kuo-feng; how many Chinese forecast the rise of Jimmy Carter?) The Chinese leaders have long demonstrated a striking capacity to adopt policies at sharp variance with their public posture, which often confuses governments trying to deal with China. Chinese politics are often carried on in secrecy, and issues and power struggles are decided by shifting combinations of personal ties, ideology, and interest groups, while information about them reaches the outside world largely by elliptical allusions difficult to decipher. Furthermore, Chinese politics have been notably unstable at the top levels in the past ten years. The purges of Liu Shao-chi, Lin Piao, Teng Hsiao-ping and the deaths of Chou En-lai and Mao Tse-tung have plunged China into a struggle for power as well as over fundamental issues, which raises important questions about the country's future stability, direction, and its ability to follow a consistent course.

In the United States, differences between the Executive and Congress, and between government policies and private sector activities, often makes it difficult to tell who speaks—or acts— for America. Moreover, the Watergate-enforced resignation of Richard Nixon, Gerald Ford's status as an unelected president, and the constraints created by the 1976 national election before the advent of the Carter Administration led to a reluctance on the part of the government of the United States to make new departures in foreign policy—or even to move ahead along the previously charted path in its China policy.

Sino-American relations probably are at a watershed. There appears to be a Chinese disappointment over the slow pace of normalization in U.S.-PRC relations, and perhaps a general worry or suspicion that the Taiwan issue may prove unresolvable. Not that the Chinese leaders expect—or want?—to regain control of Taiwan soon, but they do want U.S.-ROC diplomatic and defense ties cut once and for all. Yet even those most disappointed over continued U.S. ties to Taiwan probably recognize that the rapprochement with the United States reduced the possibility of a formalized two-China solution.

In this book the authors examine not only where the two countries stand in the normalization process—and the outlook for completing it—but also the consequences of a failure to carry it through. (The phrase "normalization" has been used in so many Sino-American communiqués and statements that it has become part of the vocabulary of the subject despite its vagueness and the unwarranted implication it carries that all will be well between the two countries once the process is completed.) The possibility of failure must be taken seriously. According to a poll taken late in 1975, 61 percent of the American people want to normalize relations with Peking, but 70 percent want to do so without breaking relations with Taiwan.[4] China is clearly not the divisive issue in American politics that it was in the past, when the search for those officials who "lost" China—and the power of the China lobby—drove talented men from office and doomed American policies to rigidity. At the same time, there is little positive political mileage to be gained from further advances toward normalization—although a major setback in Sino-American relations would have domestic political costs for a president. In these circumstances we must examine the effects that several years of stalemate would have on the relations between China and the United States on their respective foreign policies (especially on their relations with the Soviet Union and Japan), and on world politics generally. Failure to work out a better relationship would carry heavy costs for both countries, but there are important forces in China and the United States that regard the costs of hostility as bearable and the benefits of détente as modest if not illusory.

[7]

Even if the two governments surmount the obstacles to normalization, what sort of a relationship is likely to evolve between two such different societies? History has many examples of the most diverse societies cooperating internationally in the face of a common danger, but will *these* two societies be able to do so over a prolonged period? The present leaders of both countries probably view the bedrock of the Sino-American relationship as their common agreement that the Soviet Union is the major antagonist of each country. Yet Washington and Peking are pursuing strikingly different policies toward Moscow. Chinese leaders have become increasingly worried since 1974 about the U.S.-Soviet détente. Despite the setbacks that the Soviet-American détente has experienced in this period, Peking continues to attack it as illusory and dangerous. Americans have come to expect less from détente with the U.S.S.R. than they did a few years ago, but they are not inclined to abandon the basic policy.

A few words now about the chapters that follow. A basic determinant of Chinese policy is the view Chinese leaders hold of the international system generally, and of the American role in it. This topic, and its consequences for Chinese foreign policy, are the subject of the following chapter. Akira Iriye presents an overview of the evolution of Chinese perceptions of the international environment since the Communists' rise to power. Next, the nature and importance of bilateral Sino-American relations, and how they influence and are influenced by each country's relations with third parties and by world affairs generally, receive careful examination. Trade and cultural exchanges, the two most significant aspects of the bilateral relationship, are analyzed in separate chapters, which also place these activities in their larger settings. Alexander Eckstein appraises the shifting role of foreign trade in Chinese economic and foreign policy, the trend of Sino-American trade, and the consequent policy issues facing each country. Lucian Pye examines not only the official cultural exchange programs and the issues their management poses for two such different governments, but the underlying cultural traits of each society, which both facilitate and hamper cultural exchanges. Because the Taiwan issue remains the major immediate obstacle to better Sino-American relations, Ralph Clough appraises it from the standpoints of the Chinese and American roles in the dispute and also in terms of the ability of the people in Taiwan to shape their destiny. He examines the key issues and the requirements for dealing with the matter in a way that will be acceptable, if not wholly satisfactory, to all parties concerned.

The book concludes with my chapter assessing the role China has played in American foreign policy in recent decades and an analysis of the issues and choices the United States faces in its policy toward China, as seen in the larger context of America's foreign policy tasks in the years ahead. Although our chapters are primarily analytical, they also set forth policy recommendations which the authors believe would contribute to the gradual establishment of a mutually beneficial Sino-American relationship to replace the tragic hostility of the past.

NOTES

1. Stanley Karnow, "Chinese Through Rose-Tinted Glasses," *The Atlantic Monthly,* Vol. 232, No. 4 (October 1973), p. 74.

2. For a perceptive analysis of the varying Chinese responses, see Michel Oksenberg and Steven Goldstein, "China's Political Spectrum," *Problems of Communism,* March-April 1974, pp. 1-13.

3. Michael B. Yahuda, "Chinese Foreign Policies After the Victories in Indochina," *The World Today,* July 1975, p. 298.

4. *The New York Times,* November 6, 1975.

[TWO]

The United States in Chinese Foreign Policy

Akira Iriye

Events in the People's Republic of China before and since Mao's death, and the changes that are bound to take place in the near future, make it more than ever necessary to develop a historical perspective to understand the meaning of contemporary Sino-American relations. An essay on Chinese affairs written at the time of Chou En-lai's death in January 1976 would have been quite different from one written after the rise to power of the hitherto obscure Hua Kuo-feng and the fall of Teng Hsiao-p'ing, but it in turn would have been out of date after Mao Tse-tung died and attacks on "the gang of four" began. One hesitates to make any systematic analysis, let alone confident predictions, about Chinese politics when the Chinese leaders themselves seem unsure of its direction. Perhaps all that can safely be said is that whatever individual or group leads China will have as a major preoccupation the establishment of an aura of legitimacy and the extension of government authority throughout the land.

Nevertheless, China as a nation-state is more than the sum of its factions, cliques, and leading personalities. Just as preoccupation with a presidential election in the United States would mislead observers of the American scene about continuities and long-range trends in the country's domestic politics and foreign policy, so fascination with the day-to-day changes in personal and factional fortunes could cause one to lose sight of the issues and challenges that confront China regardless of such vicissitudes. These problems do not vanish as swiftly as individual leaders or "gangs" seem to do.

Some of the issues, in fact, have persisted for more than a century. The most fundamental one has been the problem of development: how best to organize the national community in order to undertake economic growth. Within this broad question, which China shares with all other countries, the Chinese have had to grapple with specific issues that have arisen because of the pecularities of its international position since the nineteenth century, surrounded as it has been by countries (Russia, Japan, India, etc.) at different stages of growth, each with its own ambitions and views as to the use it could make of China's resources. Even countries not contiguous to China—the United States, Britain, etc.—have tried to incorporate it into what they regard to be a viable international political and economic order, with the result that the Chinese have had to react to external pressures more often than they have been able to generate initiatives of their own.

These are fundamental challenges that confront China's leadership, beside which the immediate questions of who is to emerge as leader, which faction is to stage a comeback, and so on, sound almost banal. Domestic politics, of course, will be central to the extent that different individuals and groups may try to cope with these challenges according to their differing perceptions of them and how their solutions may in turn help them consolidate their power base. This type of linkage has, as is to be expected, a story of its own in any society. Events in 1976, many of them unanticipated by even the most astute outside observers, should caution us, however, against assuming too formalistic a pattern of such linkages. While the turmoil continues, it seems better to try to discern long-term trends and distill certain characteristics of Chinese perception and behavior—which this essay attempts to do.

The Chinese leadership, whatever form it may take, will continue to be faced by the same kinds of foreign policy questions their predecessors faced. They will have to define anew China's international status and role at a time when U.S.-Soviet relations appear to be entering a period of uncertainty, when the industrial countries have not completely recovered from the worst economic crisis since the 1930s, and when nations are intensifying their determination to claim larger segments of the skies, oceans, and subsoil resources as their exclusive jurisdiction. They will have to establish a position for China vis-à-vis both the industrial and the developing nations. They will have to respond to periodic Soviet overtures for better relations, which have been more frequent since the death of Mao, but which represent one of the most complex and contentious issues in Chinese foreign policy. Toward the United States in particular, they will have to clarify their stand on the degree of economic, political, and cultural interdependence that should exist between the two countries. They will also have to decide how rigid—or how flexible—to be in insisting that the "one China" formula be the basis of their formal dealings with Washington, insisting on American recognition of Peking as the government of all China, including Taiwan.

Some of these specific problems are analyzed extensively by other essays in this book. The main aim of this chapter is to provide a historical framework for the discussion of contemporary issues. It does so by focusing on the changing Chinese perceptions of "the international situation," as they so often refer to it. (There have been, of course, differences among Chinese leaders on these matters over the past several decades, and such contrasting views are highlighted when they involve important policy choices.) It seems useful to examine these perceptions because historically the Chinese have always been acutely conscious of their position in the world. This is true of any people, but the case of the Chinese is unique because of their strong historical consciousness and because their Marxist-Leninist-Maoist view of the modern world presupposes a certain role for China to play in the unfolding drama of international politics. Even when they act on specific issues between them and another country, they have generally been concerned with defining those issues not only as bilateral questions of diplomacy but as evidence that world history has reached a certain stage. Thus their approach to Sino-American relations is quite often couched in the language of historical development and of trends in the world arena. They recognize, of course, that the United States, like the Soviet Union and other countries, plays an often decisive role in international relations, but they tend to put their emphasis on the system as a whole rather than on its constituent elements. That is to say, they are prone to treat U.S.-Chinese relations not in a strictly bilateral but in a broad international framework.

Thus it is useful to consider some of the ways in which the Chinese have perceived the international system. Like all studies of images, unqualified generalizations are risky, but without some attempt at generalizing, any discussion of

[14]

specific questions would in itself be of little long-term usefulness. If this essay appears to slight the relationship between domestic politics and foreign policy, it is in part because of the lack of sufficient data, but also because it is believed that in a short essay like this, preoccupation with too many exceptions and details will distort the overall picture. With this caveat, one may consider several stages in recent Chinese perceptions of the world through a working chronology that subdivides the years since the 1930s into six periods:

1. The war years
2. 1945-49
3. 1949-55
4. 1955-63
5. 1963-71
6. 1971-76

These periods, of course, were preceded by nearly two centuries of contact between the two countries, a tradition which constitutes one part of American and Chinese consciousness today. But this is not the place to discuss that tradition. Suffice it to recall that before the 1930s U.S.-Chinese relations had been overwhelmingly informal and indirect: informal in the sense that individual roles and personal encounters between Chinese and Americans were far more important than official diplomacy; indirect in the sense that images like American wealth and China's markets played more significant roles in shaping their respective opinions than direct dealings with one another. Even so, one theme should be stressed. Both China and the United States tended to relate to one another in the larger context of Asian international relations, and particularly within the tripartite relationship of Japan, China, and the United States. The context was defined by the Chinese as imperialist diplomacy on the part of the industrial countries, which appeared united in their determination to preserve their vested interests in underdeveloped regions of the world. At the same time, the Chinese perceived potential conflicts between more advanced countries like the

[15]

United States and a less industrialized power such as Japan. But even the latter showed little tolerance of China's own economic development and political modernization.

Thus, starting at least from the time of the Russo-Japanese War (1904-1905), some Chinese officials began to view American capitalism as a possible counterweight to Japanese ambitions. They proposed to invite American loans and investments to undermine Japan's monopolistic hold on Manchuria, a pattern of thinking that continued all the way to the 1930s. Kuomintang diplomacy was essentially one that aimed at utilizing the economic and political resources of the United States in order to frustrate Japan's aggressive attempt to create an Asian regional block to satisfy its needs. In contrast, some Chinese leaders, notably Wang Ching-wei, were convinced that such a strategy was inherently false since it subordinated the interests of China to those of America, a country which was going through a serious economic crisis of its own in the 1930s. Rather, they insisted, China should tie its destiny to Japan's in order to effect political unity and economic development.

No matter which side was taken, it is noticeable that the Chinese failed on the whole to develop a vision of harmonious relations among the three countries. These relations were generally seen as an ongoing contest between one of them against the other two, *on the assumption* that their interests could not be reconciled so long as China remained weak and undeveloped. The Chinese attitude toward the United States was a function of their perception of the trends in U.S.-Japanese relations, which, in turn, were seen as a reflection of the advanced countries' intense rivalry to restructure international politics in the wake of the world economic crisis.

[16]

The War Years

During the Sino-Japanese War (1937-45), many National-ists and Communists were eager to make use of American resources to block Japan's subjugation of China. A minority of Chinese believed the United States was, if anything, more selfish and less sensitive to Asian aspirations than was Japan, and justified their alliance with the latter as the best means for undertaking Chinese development. The bankruptcy of this third group was due not only to its mismanagement of areas under its control but more fundamentally to the implausibility of its vision of a postwar Asia to be developed with Japanese resources. The Nationalists and the Communists accepted American power as a basic ingredient of postwar Asia politics, and they tried to make use of that power as they sought to keep Japanese militarism in check and devoted themselves to the task of gaining control of China.

There was, it should be noted, a gap between such a perception and the actuality of American policy and strategy. It is true that the United States was intent upon constructing a postwar system of international relations in Asia that was to prevent the resurgence of Japan's pan-Asianist imperialism. But this system was visualized as basically America's unilateral construction. The United States would be the leading Asian-Pacific power, with naval bases throughout the Pacific Ocean and its troops occupying Japan. It would, of course, recognize the importance of the Soviet Union, Great Britain, and China as the other principal postwar Asian powers; but unlike Europe, where the future shape of the American-Soviet-British relationship was under constant discussion throughout the war, in Asia the quadrilateral relationship was never clearly defined. Little initiative was taken by Washington to consult with London, Moscow, or Chungking about their mutual cooperation after the war. In fact, the thrust of American planning for postwar Asia was to ensure peace, stability, and development of the region primarily through the preponderant military and economic power of the United States. Specific patterns of bilateral or multilateral ties with other countries were less important.[1]

Many Chinese Nationalists and Communists, for their part, were strongly interested in having the United States play a key role in Asian politics after Japan's defeat, understanding well the enormous implications of a continued American presence in Asia. The Nationalists wanted to maintain the American alliance so as to prevent Soviet and British penetration after the war. The Communists, too, assumed that the United States would remain an active Asian power, but they also believed this would not conflict with Soviet influence in postwar Asia. Their ideological affiliation with the Soviet Union and concurrent receptivity to economic and political ties with the United States revealed that they had—at least briefly—a vision of a workable trilateral relationship, an international framework for China's unification and development (under the Communist leadership, of course) which would draw inspiration and support both from Russia and America. It may be said that such a vision, which can be discerned in Mao's wartime speeches, was more articulate about the postwar Asian international system than the views being formulated by American officials.[2]

1945-49: THE CHANGE OF REGIMES IN CHINA

After Japan's defeat, the United States continued to act

unilaterally in Asia, most notably by controlling the policy for the occupation of Japan. The policy of unilateralism reflected the idea, as General Douglas MacArthur said, that America had a unique role to play in the Asia-Pacific region where "great events of the next thousand years would transpire." If the Americans were able to bring to the billion people residing in this area "the blessings of freedom and of a higher standard of living," they would "fundamentally alter the course of world history." [3] Such a vision, which harkened back to the nineteenth century, did not call for special ties or power-political arrangements with other countries. Although the United States did occasionally work with its wartime allies about the occupation of Japan or the status of Korea, it refrained from seeking a new basis for diplomacy in Asia, in contrast to Europe where it would soon be "creating" an international system to cope with postwar developments. Toward China there was no departure from the state of affairs during the war; no new initiatives were taken to consolidate ties with Kuomintang China against the Soviet Union, or, even as the Communists were moving toward power, to deal with them in a framework of American-Soviet-Chinese cooperation as the basis for Asian peace. (The continuation of wartime arrangements did mean, of course, that Washington would deal more with the Nationalists than with the Communists.)

United States officials, to be sure, were aware of the danger of Soviet-American conflict. Already in October 1945 the Joint Intelligence Committee was predicting that Russia's foreign policy would aim at "the establishment of Soviet control over the Eurasian land mass and the strategic approaches thereto." By early November the committee had selected twenty targets in Soviet territory for attack by atomic bombs.[4] These were traditional concerns and contingency plans of the military, interested in the next hypothetical war; but preoccupation with Soviet expansionism permeated Washington's officialdom to such an extent that by the fall of 1946, when the celebrated Clifford memorandum was written, international relations had come to be perceived in terms of a global struggle for power between communism and anti-communism.[5] The struggle was viewed as a zero-sum game in which gains for one camp would automatically mean losses to the other.

This world view was necessarily applied to Asia, and the various war plans drafted at this time envisaged the use of American bases in the region in case of an attack upon Russia. Still, at least until 1949, the emphasis in U.S. policy and strategy was overwhelmingly upon Western Europe and the Middle East, and only secondarily upon North Africa, Latin America, and the Far East. In various policy memoranda of the Joint Chiefs of Staff and the National Security Council, one often finds explicit statements to the effect that American policy in the Far East was to be subordinate to the needs elsewhere. There was a gap, in other words, between perception and policy in America's Cold War diplomacy in Asia. Despite the globalism in its perceptions of the Cold War, American policy did little to prevent the Communist take-over of China in the late 1940s. Nor did the United States pursue a calculated Cold War policy either in Korea or in Southeast Asia. It did remain the dominant force in Japan, but this had little to do with Cold War diplomacy, for it was a continuation of a strategy decided upon earlier.

The American retreat from the Asian mainland after the failure of the Marshall Mission was a disaster for the Chinese Nationalists; for them, it implied the evaporation of their hopes for a U.S.-Chinese entente against Russia, as well as for their victory in the civil war. For the Chinese Communists, on the other hand, the retreat should have been welcome, but they, too, became bitterly estranged from America. The reason was that initially they failed to be persuaded that the United States meant to reduce its commitments in China. Instead, the Communists castigated American intervention in the Chinese civil war, denouncing it as an attempt to "subjugate the Chinese people and turn China into a complete satellite of the United States," as Chou En-lai said in December 1946. Chiang Kai-shek was pictured as a man who was selling his country to American imperialism.

It is difficult to determine, however, whether the Chinese Communist leaders really believed that the United States was intending to use all means to support the Nationalists and make China an American protectorate. It is well known that during 1946-47 there was serious disagreement among them about strategy in the civil war precisely because they were unsure of the degree of American determination to support the Nationalists.[6] But the key to the Communists' attitude was their perception of world trends after the war. Now that the anti-fascist coalition had triumphed, they saw international politics as an arena for the struggle between democratic and anti-democratic forces. The latter, led by the United States, faced the worldwide movements against imperialism and oppression. Regardless of America's ambitions and capabilities to impose its will, the Chinese Communists, according to this analysis, should align themselves with democratic forces both within and outside China. The Soviet Union was only one such force, and not even the most important, for the Communists sensed Russia's reluctance to come to their aid at the risk of provoking the United States into a third world war. For this reason, they emphasized the need to identify their aspirations and interests with general aspirations for freedom, while at the same time relying *primarily* upon their own resources for domestic reconstruction and development. This was clearly a shift away from wartime assumptions about turning to advanced industrial countries for aid. As Chou said in 1947, "the Chinese Communists will henceforth work out their own problems without mediation by the Soviet Union, Great Britain, the United States, or any other foreign country."[7]

After 1947, with both Moscow and Washington formally declaring the onset of the Cold War, the Chinese Communists began stressing the theme of "leaning to one side," emphasizing the impossibility of standing between the two camps. Specialists disagree on the exact meaning of this phrase, but it is clear that, given the Cold War tensions, the Chinese were counting on some Soviet aid as well as trying to prevent Russia from sacrificing China's interests in its strategy toward the United States in Europe and the Middle East. It was also imperative to demonstrate China's loyalty to the Soviet model of development when the world seemed divided between those who followed the American road to capitalism and those who opposed it. At this time, moreover, the Chinese viewed the United States as intent upon restoring Japanese militarism by moderating its occupation policy and encouraging Japan's economic recovery. Japan could turn into an advance base for U.S.-Japanese collusion at the expense of China. One way of preventing this was to insist on a Japanese peace treaty which must be negotiated by all the parties concerned, including, of course, Russia and China. Another was to enter into a formal alliance with the Soviet Union against Japan and its supporters. In all these efforts, one sees the Chinese Communist leadership's keen interest in the developing international situation.[8]

1949-55: Hot and Cold War

In retrospect, the Sino-Soviet negotiations which culminated in their treaty of alliance (February 1950) already contained seeds of deep suspicion between Peking and Moscow. To the United States government, however, the treaty appeared as further evidence that China had fallen to the Soviet camp. It was around this time that the United States began to pursue a more systematic Asian policy. After 1949-50, as indicated by the recently declassified documents of the National Security Council, the United States government came to view Asia as a main theater of the Cold War in need of a comprehensive strategy like that for Europe and the Middle East. American security and interests in India, Southeast Asia, Korea, and Japan were now seen as interrelated, and policy toward China became part of the overall strategy toward the Communist bloc. The importance of Japan as a dependable base was reconfirmed, and Southeast Asia and Korea became particularly crucial because of their relevance to Japanese economic interests and security. However, this new strategy, adopted by the National Security Council on December 30, 1949 (as NSC 48/2), was not publicized. Instead, the famous speech by Secretary of State Dean Acheson on January 12, 1950, gave the impression of writing off Korea as lying outside the American "defense perimeter." Thus the North Korean invasion of South Korea and the swift U.S. response caused surprise around the world. American policy before June 25 was based upon the assumption or judgment that the Communist states would not resort to direct warfare—and that view was proven wrong by North Korea. Thus American policy after June 25 was in accord with NSC 48/2, as was the decision to support the Bao Dai regime in

Indochina, which preceded the outbreak of the Korean War. The Cold War in Asia had now turned into a hot war.

It should be noted, however, that the United States continued to view the Korean conflict largely in terms of U.S.-Soviet relations. As General Omar Bradley, chairman of the Joint Chiefs of Staff, told Secretary of Defense Louis Johnson on July 10, "if major USSR combat units should at any time during military operations in the Korean area of hostilities engage or clearly indicate their intention of engaging in hostilities against U.S. and/or friendly forces, the United States should prepare to minimize its commitment in Korea." Otherwise, in case of a world war the Soviet Union would be able to exploit "excessive commitments of United States military forces and resources in those areas of operations which would not be decisive." [9] Throughout the Korean War, moreover, the United States regarded the Soviet Union as the party with whom it would have to deal to bring the hostilities to an end. This, of course, was what happened after the U.S.S.R.'s appeal for cease-fire talks in April 1951. Thus, despite the persistence of the global Cold War, the two powers were finding it prudent to remain in touch to discuss key international issues so as to avoid an actual war between them. Gradually, especially after Stalin's death in 1953, they began to recognize that they might be speaking the same language, the language which came to be known as peaceful coexistence. The summit conference of 1955 in this sense marked the end of one chapter of the Cold War, though not of the Cold War itself.[10]

Soviet-American negotiations served to separate U.S.-Chinese relations from U.S.-U.S.S.R. relations. From the Chinese perspective, the United States was now a greater menace than ever before. While pre-1949 attacks on American imperialism had been in large part a rhetorical device, a product of a certain world-view, after 1950 the United States came to be seen as an actual threat to Chinese security and independence. The separate treaty between Japan and America in 1951, coupled with the 1952 mutual security pact, confirmed for China that the two were now closely allied in Asia, and that the United States was definitely interested in restoring Japanese military power. America was also the one power that stood in the way of completing national unification through the liberation of Taiwan. Through its sending the Seventh Fleet into the Taiwan Straits in June 1950, its support of the Kuomintang regime on the island, its stationing of troops there, and its security treaty with Nationalist China, the United States was, from Peking's point of view, forcefully occupying part of Chinese territory. American bombings of the Korean-Manchurian border during the Korean War, the threat of the use of nuclear weapons by the United States toward the end of the war, the offshore islands crisis in 1955, and the infiltration of Nationalist agents into the China mainland, all added up to a picture of America as the major menace to China. Furthermore, the formation of the Southeast Asia Treaty Organization (SEATO) in 1954, as well as the network of bilateral security treaties with various Asian countries, especially Japan and South Korea, confirmed for the Chinese their view that the United States harbored hostile intentions against the new regime.

In order to cope with this critical situation, the Chinese leaders needed to reassess the changing world situation. At one level, they still held to a bipolar image and believed in the solidarity of Sino-Soviet relations. China needed Soviet support, especially its nuclear capabilities, to repulse an American attack, and the Chinese thought they deserved such assistance. As Mao Tse-tung later recalled, Chinese participation in the Korean conflict against American forces enhanced Peking's credibility with Moscow, which was now more willing to treat China as an equal.[11] In 1954 Khrushchev agreed to end the joint Sino-Soviet companies Stalin had insisted on establishing in 1950, and also to abandon Soviet base rights in Port Arthur.

But at the same time, as Robert Simmons and others have shown, Soviet conduct during the Korean War must have convinced the Chinese that, despite their 1950 treaty, the Soviet Union could not entirely be depended upon to come to the aid of China automatically.[12] The gradual loss of confidence in the value of the Soviet alliance was certainly a factor behind the renewed interest in creating a coalition of Asian countries that would include even neutral states like India. This did not cause any immediate divergence between Soviet and Chinese policies, for the Soviet Union, in pursuit of a peaceful coexistence policy, was also eager to befriend the Asian countries. However, this policy had special significance for the Chinese. The five principles of peace, enunciated by Chou En-lai in India in 1954, were designed to win the support of these countries, not necessarily to make them China's military allies against the United States but to demonstrate the solidarity of Asians against hostile American intentions. The Bandung Conference of April 1955 went a step beyond these preliminary moves in that African as well as Asian delegates participated. Usually seen as an expression of Communist China's peaceful coexistence diplomacy, the conference should probably be regarded, at least in part, as China's answer to the developing U.S.-U.S.S.R. understanding on the basis of the global status quo. In other words, the Soviet-American Cold War had its own momentum and history. By 1955 the worst phase of that conflict—exemplified by the expression in NSC 68 (April 1950) that the two countries were actually engaged in war—had passed, although such episodes as the 1962 Cuban missile crisis indicated that it still contained serious dangers.

1955-63: Shifting Responses to the Emerging Soviet-American Relationship

The years between the end of the Korean War and the Sino-American détente in the early 1970s constitute a unified period in terms of the Cold War between the People's Republic of China and the United States. For nearly two decades, the two countries maintained only the most tenuous of relations through ambassadorial talks at Geneva and Warsaw and through limited individual contacts. There was virtually no formal trade or cultural relationship between Peking and Washington.

Within this broad rubric of non-relationship, different periodizations can be proposed, but one useful division would be between the years before and after 1963. This periodization might seem arbitrary in terms of Chinese domestic politics or of purely bilateral Sino-American relations. But, to the extent, as argued above, that China's policy toward the United States reflected its perception of the international system, the partial nuclear test-ban treaty between the United States and the Soviet Union in 1963 was a landmark of major significance, the culmination of a period that may be dated back to the U.S.-Soviet summit conference of 1955 and to the Twentieth Congress of the Soviet Communist Party in 1956. During this period, especially after Mao's visit to Moscow in 1957 and Khrushchev's visit to Peking the following year, the Chinese leaders came to view the United States and the Soviet Union as intent upon pursuing a policy of peaceful coexistence. The 1963 test-ban treaty confirmed Chinese views that the two superpowers now had a mutually recognized stake in maintaining the nuclear status quo and preventing third countries from challenging their pre-eminence in world politics.

This was an ominous development in Chinese eyes. They

recognized that even as the United States after 1955 talked of peace in the world, it refused to depart from the policy of ostracizing China in the international community. In fact, after the Korean War the United States had come to focus on the People's Republic of China as the most dangerous (because in its view the most reckless) adversary in Asia. The Cold War in that region now primarily connoted Sino-American antagonism rather than conflict between the United States and the Soviet Union. Moreover, in overall American strategy, Asia assumed greater importance than previously, and the United States stepped up its support of non-Communist regimes in Southeast Asia, while encouraging Japan and South Korea to reconcile their differences and become more closely linked to the Asian security system to check Chinese expansionism. American policy may not have consciously differentiated between Peking and Moscow, but the general effect amounted to such differentiation. The Cold War came increasingly to mean American opposition to Chinese, rather than Russian, expansion.

Such a development might have induced the Chinese to consolidate ties with Russia. They decided, however, that it would be better to take their own initiatives rather than to identify China's fate with that of the Soviet Union, and work out the best strategy to struggle against U.S. imperialism. The rejection of a close alliance with Russia was in part related to changes within China. In late 1955 Mao Tse-tung called on the Chinese people to step up their task of constructing a socialist country. He launched the "Hundred Flowers" campaign in 1956, and a year later an ideological offensive had to be initiated, designed to eradicate right-wing, counterrevolutionary forces which seemed to want to perpetuate bourgeois influences in China. Mao and his followers would now stress radical programs for speedily establishing a socialist state. The

"Great Leap Forward" was their policy to utilize China's huge population for economic development; and people's communes, established in 1958, were visualized as an effective instrument for organizing the masses. Implicit in all these programs was the conviction that the Chinese had the correct answer to the problem of building a socialist country, that they, rather than the Russians, were the true Marxist revolutionaries. While this view was by no means universally held within China, and while the grandiose goals of the Great Leap Forward soon had to be abandoned, these internal changes had the effect of exacerbating Chinese-Russian relations and magnifying their differences. The various shifts in directions after 1955, and especially the failure of the Great Leap Forward, also brought Mao's personal authority into serious question.

There was a brief moment, it is true, during 1955-56, when a moderate foreign policy, exemplified by the Bandung Conference and Chou En-lai's June 1956 speech (talking of the peaceful liberation of Taiwan), was enunciated with much fanfare. Scholars differ over the importance of these Chinese moves. Was Peking merely trying to strike a peaceful pose? Was it trying to disrupt American attempts to encircle China with anti-Communist alliances backed by United States military strength? [13] Or was it making a serious attempt to determine whether a less hostile Sino-American relationship was possible? No one can be sure. Moreover, as William Barnds points out in Chapter VI, the Chinese moves elicited no significant American response, and United States policy toward China—in contrast to its policy toward the Soviet Union—continued to be based upon the assumption that the Communist regime might be a passing phenomenon rather than on negotiating from strength. But in my view the key element in these Chinese moves was to assert China's role as

[29]

the champion of Asian and African countries. This reflected a gradually developing self-confidence that China could chart its own course instead of following the Russian lead. The view that a worldwide struggle against U.S. imperialism was feasible was buttressed after 1957 when the Soviet Union launched the Sputnik and Mao declared that "the east wind" was prevailing over the "west wind." If the Russians hesitated to accept such a perception as the basis for their policy, the Chinese would then seize the initiative. Thus, Chinese policy toward the United States tended to be further radicalized; it was couched more than ever before in the framework of cultural and ideological warfare.

As is well known, such assertiveness alarmed, even horrified, the Soviet leaders, who opposed Peking's "adventuristic" attacks on the offshore islands in 1958 and refused, in 1959, to provide further nuclear technology to China. Russian technicians and engineers working on a huge range of development projects were withdrawn in 1960, forcing the Chinese to rely upon the principle of "self-help." These events brought about an open clash between the leadership of the two countries. In January 1962 Mao Tse-tung declared that the Soviet leadership was now in the hands of revisionists, who demonstrated that even in a socialist society bourgeois elements could re-emerge. Men like Liu Shao-ch'i and Teng Hsiao-p'ing did not endorse such a harsh view of the Soviet Union, but they could not put the brakes on the deteriorating relationship between the two countries. As far as Mao and his supporters were concerned, Russian behavior in the world seemed no better than American, and they began to stress China's opposition to *ta-kuo chu-i* (superpower-ism).

Such perceptions dictated that China try to prevent its isolation in a world subject to the dangers of nuclear war. To China, the United States appeared willing to use atomic bombs to establish control of the world for its monopoly capitalism, while the Soviet Union was becoming less and less interested in resisting it. (The United States was willing to consider the use of nuclear weapons during the Quemoy-Matsu crisis of 1958.) In his speeches Mao Tse-tung frankly expressed the view that as many as half the Chinese population might be killed through the imperialists' use of nuclear weapons. For these reasons, it was more than ever imperative to establish China's position as the leader of the forces of nationalism throughout the world. As Mao said in September 1958, there were three contending forces in the world: imperialism, nationalism, and communism.[14] The latter two were potential allies against the first. Areas controlled by nationalism were the vast territories covering Asia, Africa, the Middle East, and Latin America. Leaders in these countries might be tied to American imperialism, but their people truly desired peace and opposed America's attempts to dominate them.

Thus the basic contradiction in the world, Mao said, was between imperialism and nationalism. The United States was likely to wage war against nationalistic forces first before turning to the invasion of socialist countries. This, in fact, would be a welcome thing for China, since it would ensure the support of nationalistic forces in its struggle with the United States. It should be noted that Mao was making these remarks during the height of the offshore islands crisis in 1958. Attacks on Quemoy and Matsu, while an expression of the long-standing aspiration to unify the whole of China, were also designed to demonstrate that China could act independently of the wishes of the Soviet leadership. Indeed, the Chinese were testing both the latter's degree of commitment to the defense of nationalism as well as Moscow's loyalty to its major ally. Because, as expected, the Russians refused to support Peking, the Chinese could view their clashes with the United States

[31]

over the islands as an instance of the global confrontation between imperialism and nationalism, a confrontation that came to define for the Chinese the basic characteristic of international affairs. Bilateral relations between China and America were far less significant than the worldwide configurations of these two forces, though President Kennedy's hints that he was exploring the possibility of a "two-China" solution brought forth bitter Chinese denuciations.[15]

Perceptions and reasoning of this sort about imperialism and nationalism were behind China's stress by the early 1960s on the "intermediate zone," the countries which were neither imperialist nor socialist. Such emphasis was dictated by the need to picture the world crisis in a most favorable light from the Chinese point of view at a time when China was still struggling to recover from the failure of the Great Leap Forward and its loss of Soviet support. The key was to isolate the United States through assuming leadership of the countries in the intermediate zone. The ultimate weapon against American imperialism, Mao often asserted, was the people in those countries. (The Sino-Indian border clashes of 1959 were an embarrassment from the standpoint of such a strategy. However, the Chinese first tried to take care of this difficulty by making a serious attempt to compromise the dispute in April 1960 when Chou En-lai visited New Delhi. Nehru's refusal to compromise, followed by the heightened tension which led to the 1962 border war, caused China to draw a distinction between the Indian people and leaders, accusing the latter of abandoning neutralism and turning to America and Russia for support.) [16]

The more ambitious the United States was to extend its power to Asia, Africa, the Middle East, and Latin America, the more inevitably it would encounter their people's fierce opposition. Thus the very power of the United States contained the seeds of its ultimate destruction. This fundamental contradiction between America and the intermediate zone would ensure China's survival and development, according to Peking's perceptions at the time. The awareness of the close links between international politics in Asia and elsewhere enabled the Communist leadership to conceive a global strategy that was not dependent upon Soviet military support. China could cope with the perceived menace of American imperialism by obtaining third world support; conversely, China could assist the countries of the intermediate zone by continuing to oppose American ambitions in Asia. In any case, confronted with Soviet and American hostility, the Chinese leaders felt they had little choice but to rely upon such a course.

1963-71: Against Imperialism, Revisionism and Hegemonism

The signing of the partial nuclear test-ban treaty in 1963 solidified the Chinese view of the United States and the Soviet Union as the two superpowers trying to establish world hegemony. Mao Tse-tung constantly referred to "American-Russian cooperation to control the world," and to the collusion of American imperialism and Russian revisionism. Since the United States had always represented the foremost imperialist power, the stress on its collusion with the revisionist leadership in Russia was a prominent feature in this period. The Soviet Union was seen as a socialist state which contained bourgeois, counterrevolutionary elements, just as in the world at large there were revolutionary and counterrevolutionary forces struggling for supremacy. The American imperialists, in other words, were now pictured as being assisted, explicitly or implicitly, by the Soviet revisionists. The test-ban treaty, from such a point of view, was an expression of great-power arrogance and selfishness. China would never join such a group of superpowers but would instead develop its own nuclear weapons to assert its independence. Its successful nuclear tests in October 1964 were hailed as an expression of China's "self-help" and its determination to break up the great powers' "nuclear monopoly."

The spectacle of Soviet-American collusion was serious. It became even more so as the Chinese leaders watched the stepped-up American involvement in Indochina while the Soviet Union began to show signs of its "social imperialism"— a phrase Chou En-lai used during the Russian invasion of Czechoslovakia in 1968. The Chinese faced a serious question whether they could afford to alienate both the United States and the Soviet Union, or whether they should temporarily concentrate on defending national rights against one super-power at a time. During the Vietnam war, the danger of American invasion of China could not be discounted. Should war with the United States come, China could be forced to turn to Russia for help on whatever terms it could get, and at the very time that the theme of self-help was being empha-sized. Whether China should continue attacks on Soviet revisionism, whether such a choice might not necessitate avoidance of open clashes with the United States—these were questions which had obvious domestic implications. Indeed, they sparked a major political and strategic debate in China in 1964-65. Mao and his followers refused to deviate from opposition both to imperialism and revisionism while Liu, Teng, P'eng Chen and other Party "bureaucrats," as well as some military leaders like Lo Jui-ch'ing, preferred a common front with Russia in the face of the deepening Vietnam conflict.

Mao and his followers were initially in the minority, and partly for this reason Mao launched an audacious movement to eradicate revisionist forces within China, known as the Great Proletarian Cultural Revolution (1965-69). Counterrevolutionaries inside China were identified with the revisionist leadership, and Mao's political foes were denounced as subservient to the Soviet Union. "Mao Tse-tung thought," a phrase which began to be used about 1960 and was invoked with regularity after 1965, became official dogma tolerating no deviation.

The intensity of the domestic struggles in China in the late 1960s gave the appearance that the country was isolating itself from international affairs, unable to devise a systematic approach to them. It is possible, however, to discern certain currents of thought among Chinese leaders which had implications for Sino-American relations. First of all, they still needed to believe in the unity of the peoples of Asia, Africa, the Middle East, and Latin America. Now more than ever before their assistance was needed because Russian cooperation had to be eschewed. These peoples' overwhelming denunciation of American action in Vietnam and Russian intervention in Czechoslovakia was publicized to indicate that China had worldwide moral (if not physical) support. As Vietnamese, Laotians, Cambodians, Palestinian Arabs, Cubans, and others appeared to be intensifying their assault upon one or the other of the superpowers, China could, at least symbolically, join and lead them in the struggle. (This would also help Peking in the struggle with Moscow inside the internationalist communist movement.) Moreover, Peking would support the nonalignment diplomacy of the Asian and African countries since all of them were inherently anti-imperialist.

This policy, however, was not always consistently carried out as Peking sometimes supported armed struggles by rebellious forces in India, Burma, Indonesia, and other countries—attempts which in almost all instances provoked fierce opposition of the leaders in these countries and militated against the theme of encouraging global nationalism against superpower imperialism. Nonetheless, Mao continued to insist in 1970 that China would champion the small countries' nationalism against the oppressive ambitions of the great powers.[17]

The second theme which emerged during this period extended the first in a different way: it was the idea that anti-imperialist forces were not confined to the non-Western countries. Mao Tse-tung often suggested that the imperialists and their revisionist friends (mostly in Russia) comprised only ten percent of the world's population. The remaining ninety percent were revolutionaries, actual and potential, all yearning to be liberated from the yoke of great-power oppression. In expressing this perception, Chinese policy at times tried to appeal to all forces opposed to the handful of imperialists and revisionists. It sought to exploit the differences among Western nations and promote anti-American orientations of their governments. Not surprisingly, the "intermediate zone" in Chinese perception was expanded to include not only the less advanced countries but also the industrial nations of the West which opposed the United States.[18] The most notable example was de Gaulle's France, with which China established diplomatic relations in 1964. Membership among the disaffected was open-ended. In 1970, Canada and Italy formally joined the group of countries which acted independently of the United States by recognizing the Peking government. It would seem that by then China's identification with Asia, Africa, and Latin America had become sufficiently diluted so that almost anything was considered possible, short of reconciliation with American imperialism. Such a development obviously reflected the growing awareness, made more acute by the 1969 clashes with Soviet forces along the Ussuri River, that the Soviet Union now presented the most immediate threat to Chinese sovereignty. The enunciation of the so-called Brezhnev Doctrine and the Soviet Union's Asian Collective Security Plan—the latter clearly aimed at encircling and containing China as far as the Chinese leaders were concerned—only added to Chinese apprehensions.

Third, after 1969, as Chinese politics entered a critical phase, apparently involving a power struggle between Lin Piao's supporters (mostly in the People's Liberation Army) and Chou En-lai's (the "pragmatists" in the Party), the second theme was further developed to pave the way for a less belligerent attitude toward the United States. (A few hesitant overtures had been made as early as 1968, but they had little immediate impact.) As Mao Tse-tung declared in May 1970, although the American imperialists and their followers had to be resolutely opposed, even within the United States there were forces struggling against imperialism. There were "revolutionary mass movements" not only by blacks but also by white Americans, who were heroically fighting against Nixon's "fascism." Chou and his supporters made use of such a perception to oust from power Lin and his followers who held to a more rigid view of the United States, as well as the Soviet Union, and who justified massive military preparedness and the maintenance of a state of emergency at home.[19] The "pragmatists," on the other hand, could visualize a much more favorable international environment because revolutionary forces throughout the world, in Europe and inside the United states as well as in the less advanced areas of the world, were successfully waging a war to isolate imperialist reactionaries in America and in several other countries. The latter might still want to throw the world into global conflagration, but the revolutionary movements everywhere would prevent such adventurism. It was but a step from such a perception to the view that United States imperialism was sufficiently weakened so that it no longer posed the most serious menace to peace. In fact, it would now be possible to adopt a new strategy toward it.

1971-76: The Search for a New Relationship

Sino-American relations entered a new phase when the two governments announced, in July 1971, that President Nixon would visit China on Chou En-lai's invitation. This startling announcement was a culmination of the developments in Chinese and American foreign policies during the preceding period. The rationale for the new initiatives toward the United States was fully explained by Chou En-lai in his numerous talks with foreign visitors and by some Party directives. What emerges from a perusal of this material is a rather opportunistic view of America. No longer was the United States seen solely as an aggressive imperialist, tied to other imperialist countries and bent upon world domination. American imperialism, in fact, was now merely an abstract notion which did not evoke specific images of aggression. Thus in a single interview with visiting Japanese newspapermen, Chou could denounce U.S. imperialism and at the same time assert that American businessmen wanted peace, and that even President Nixon could be utilized for peace.[20] Nixon's China trip was proclaimed by the Communist Party as a great victory of Maoism, as it enhanced China's "international prestige"—a rather conventional (even "bourgeois") criterion of success. Even while Chinese foreign policy was said to aim at re-establishing contact with the American people, party propaganda stressed

[38]

the need to deal first of all with President Nixon since without his cooperation there could be no resumption of friendly relations. Such a shift in Chinese policy probably required the prestige of Mao and Chou because of the long period of Sino-American hostility. The United States was now seen and described within a conventional framework, as just another country, not as the embodiment of evil imperialism.

The struggle against U.S. imperialism, it is true, was still a theme in Chinese pronouncements in this period, but Mao Tse-tung was depicted as the wise leader who made use of the contradictions between American imperialism and Soviet revisionism. The language used was no different from the traditional balance-of-power concept. Thus the fact that the Soviet Union was extremely disturbed over the Sino-American rapprochement was said to demonstrate the correctness of Chinese foreign policy; it showed that the Russians were fundamentally hostile to China. Moreover, the resumption of U.S.-Chinese ties was viewed as a step in the reorientation of American imperialism away from Asia, so that the United States would concentrate its ambitions on Europe and the Middle East, thereby magnifying the contradictions between America and Russia.

Similarly, Peking reoriented its policy toward Japan in the framework of perceived changes in the international situation. On the one hand, the relative rise of Japanese power (though primarily economic) in Asia made it imperative to prevent Japan's collusion with the two superpowers. The willingness to welcome Prime Minister Tanaka's visit in 1972 was explained by the Chinese leaders as a brilliant stroke of diplomacy, since the rapprochement with China emboldened Japan toward the Soviet Union and the United States, thus further intensifying their mutual competition and contradictions. It would henceforth be impossible for Russia, America, and Japan to encircle and isolate China. At the same time, now that the U.S. position in Asia appeared to be declining because of the Vietnam fiasco, it would be in China's interest to prevent too drastic a change in power equilibrium in the region. Japan could complement the United States in maintaining a stable balance and frustrate Russian ambitions for greater power. After the end of 1971, Peking stopped denouncing the U.S.-Japanese security treaty. Even attacks on Japanese militarism, the prevention of which was given as one of the reasons for the rapprochement with America, became less and less frequent. By 1976, Chinese leaders were telling American and Japanese visitors that Peking understood that U.S.-Japanese relations took precedence over Sino-Japanese relations.

These new moves were little different from traditional power politics, indicating that after the turmoil of the Cultural Revolution China's "pragmatic" leadership, led by Chou and Teng, reverted to national-interest, as against ideological, diplomacy. It should also be noted, however, that the Chinese kept insisting they were not, and never would be, "a great power," and would continue to oppose big-power "hegemonism" by Russia and America. This was a way of defining China's role anew as that of the leader of smaller countries. As Teng Hsiao-p'ing declared at the United Nations in 1974, China would be the leader of the "third world." Unlike earlier definitions of international relations, however, the "first world" was now said to comprise the Soviet Union as well as the United States. Industrial countries other than these two now belonged to the "second world," which too could be potentially opposed to American and Soviet hegemonism.

In fact, by elevating Russia to first-world status, Chinese policy had by this time formally singled out that country as its major preoccupation. China would make use of the contradictions between the United States and the Soviet Union, as well as the latent and actual anti-hegemonist sentiments of the other two worlds, in resisting "social imperialism," a phrase which came to be used to refer to the Soviet Union. As Chou said in December 1971, the social imperialists were attempting to realize the dream of world empire which even the older "militaristic, feudalistic 'imperialism'" had been unable to achieve. Likewise, the *Jen-min Jih-pao* editorial of July 11, 1975, pointed out, Soviet social imperialism was turning Russia, a superpower, into a super-exploiter of the third world. Because of the exploitation by the two "creditor nations," a large number of developing nations were suffering from spiraling amounts of debt obligations. But these countries were persisting in their demands for independence and national liberation. In this way, China's traditional opposition to imperialism was redefined for the current world situation as resistance to big-power hegemonism. This aim could be accomplished both by identifying China with all the victims of U.S.-U.S.S.R. hegemonism and by taking advantage of the inherent contradictions in the relations of the two super-powers.

Within this broad framework, published Chinese accounts of the United States after 1971 gained some specificity now that direct contacts were being resumed, and Peking's leaders apparently considered it advisable to impart current information about American society to the Chinese people. One prominent theme was the revolutionary potential of the American masses, in particular, women, blacks, Chicanos, and laborers. For instance, in one of the few direct reports on the United States after the Nixon visit to China, a Hsin-hua reporter published a long article in *Jen-min Jih-pao* (March 9, 1972) about "the advancement of American women's revolutionary struggle." Women in the United States, it was noted, were engaged in a struggle to obtain equal rights and to oppose wars of aggression. That struggle was an important part of the American people's revolutionary movement and thus reflected their "rapid awakening." In May 1974 *Kuang-ming Jih-pao* cited a Hsin-hua report concerning the struggle of black and other minority workers in the United States against the monopoly-capitalists' class oppression. Mentioning specific instances of this struggle in Florida, Louisiana, Mississippi, Alabama, South Carolina, and elsewhere throughout 1973, the article noted that important achievements had been gained by blacks and Chicanos. Moreover, white labor unions were also credited with having assisted the minorities, so that in the future the American labor movement could be expected to gain new influences and bring about a new situation in the country. In January 1973, *Jen-min Jih-pao* cited American statistics to demonstrate that in the United States the rich were getting richer while the toiling masses, especially the blacks, were getting poorer. The result, the article noted, was the further polarization of American society. The economic crisis in the United States following the oil shock of 1973 was duly reported in China, and commentators stressed rising social instability as a consequence of economic difficulties.

All these reports gave the impression that the power of the United States was eroding, with minorities and women rising and causing domestic instability. A reader of these reports would thus expect that a revolutionary upheaval was impending in America. At the same time, the Chinese press was careful to note that the friendship between the two peoples was now more solid than ever before. Mutual visits by Americans and Chinese demonstrated that the two peoples were united in their common cause against imperialism and hegemonism. This point was underscored in constant references to the global significance of minority movements in the

United States. Blacks in America, for instance, were said to be increasingly interested in affairs in the third world, with the result that all anti-hegemonist forces in the world were becoming unified. Big-power hegemonism was often characterized as a policy of "barbaric racial discrimination."

At the same time, the stress on the rising tide of worldwide revolutionary forces and the corresponding decline of American power could cause difficulties to the extent that a balance between Russia and America was deemed to be necessary to prevent their collusion. If the United States were really as weak as alleged, the relative strength of the Soviet Union would be rather formidable, especially in view of the fact that the Chinese leaders reiterated the greater threat of Russian revisionism from the superpowers. For this reason, China would not want to envisage too weakened an America—nor one that placed much faith in Soviet-American détente. Indeed, the shifting Chinese emphasis on contention and collusion between the superpowers testifies to the difficulties Chinese leaders had in understanding and describing Soviet-American relations. A *Jen-min Jih-pao* article of July 20, 1975, talked of the two superpowers' intensifying struggle not only on land but also at sea and in the air, and described the Soviet Union's use of massive manpower and resources to extend its control over space. In contrast, the United States was pictured as losing ground in this competition because of its growingly serious economic difficulties at home. This and other articles gave the impression that the United States, because of its weakened economic position and the revolutionary upheavals brought about by the minority groups, might not be capable of coping with the ambitions of Russia's social imperialism. By implication, a healthy American economy and a correspondingly strong military posture would be reassuring as a check upon Soviet designs. For this reason the Chinese from time to time depicted the theme of American strength, emphasizing to visiting Americans that the United States should keep up its defensive capabilities.[21] Such an idea would, however, do damage to the assiduously disseminated picture of America's troubled capitalism. It remained to be seen if, and to what extent, the Chinese would try to reconcile these conflicting and dissonant themes in their perception of the United States.

CHINESE PERCEPTIONS, DOMESTIC POLITICS, AND SINO-AMERICAN RELATIONS

What this brief overview indicates is that the United States has rarely been an independent variable in Chinese foreign policy. In China's perception, relations with the United States cannot be treated in a purely bilateral framework since they make sense only in the context of the overall system of international politics in Asia and elsewhere. The Chinese recognize that the United States is a major determinant of that system, but this makes them all the more sensitive to the need to couch their policy toward America in terms of "the international environment." Another way of putting the matter is to say that in Chinese policy toward the United States anti-American (or for that matter, pro-American) slogans are far less important than China's perceived position and role in the world. "American imperialism" has been a phrase used with such monotonous regularity over the past thirty years that it hardly suffices as an indicator of Chinese policy or a guide to its future orientation. The same is true of such propaganda themes as the two peoples' "joint struggle against imperialism and war," "the traditional friendship of Chinese and Americans," and the like. The impression one gets from the statements emanating from the Chinese government and press is that America *as* America is hardly a major preoccupation of the Chinese people. Nearly twenty years ago, Harold Isaacs stated in his classic study of American images of China, *Scratches on Our Minds,* that whereas countless Americans had been fascinated with China and tried to internalize their China experiences to form coherent images of the world, this phenomenon was relatively insignificant on the Chinese side. Such an observation seems as true today as ever.

It may be argued that any country would subordinate its bilateral relationship with another state to general considerations of international politics. That is true, but some nations seem to be more (or less) concerned with bilateral ties than others. For instance, Japanese foreign policy is far more oriented toward bilateral relations with the United States than is Chinese policy. Economic, political and cultural ties between Japan and America provide the foundation of Japanese policy, whereas this would hardly be the case with Chinese policy. For the People's Republic of China, the respective roles of the two countries in the overall international system have been of more fundamental importance than issues arising in bilateral U.S.-Chinese relations.

The term "international environment" is found throughout Chinese documents, and China's attitude toward the United States is usually fitted into that context. More specifically, the Chinese envisage America's roles in the maintenance of a balance of power among the nuclear giants, in the competition among the industrial powers, or in the struggle between the latter and the third world.[22] These represent different levels of international relations as perceived by the Chinese. At the first level, that of "the hegemonist struggle" between the two superpowers, China would want the United States to check the Soviet Union so as to prevent the latter's predominance in

Asia. At the second level, Chinese expectations are ambivalent, picturing growing competition and conflict among the great economic powers, while at the same time viewing all of them as suppliers of capital and technology to the less developed. At the third level, the United States is a target of worldwide nationalism, but this is no longer a simple formulation as it used to be. While China would urge third-world peoples to resist the oppression of America and Russia, the stress has tended to be placed on opposition to the latter. Sometimes American involvement in Middle Eastern affairs, for instance, is described as an effort to strengthen the position of the United States against the Soviet Union. In all these contexts the United States *per se* is less important than the functions it is perceived to perform in the international system.

If America is not an independent variable in Chinese foreign policy, what would be its determinant factors? This essay has tried to show that China's leaders have postulated various definitions of the international system into which to fit the United States and other countries, and in every instance sought to depict China's own unique position in the world. Most notable has been the image that China is not alone in the world, that it represents, leads, or joins forces opposed to imperialism, socialist revisionism, hegemonism, and the like. Even when China's international position looked hopelessly isolated—as, for instance, during the late 1960s—efforts were made to maintain and to portray a sanguine view of China's role in these struggles. The implication is that Chinese policy toward the United States would be determined by a sense of world order and China's position in it, not primarily by bilateral questions arising between the two countries. To the extent that the Chinese leaders perceive the world in terms of Soviet ambitions, the U.S.-Russian nuclear stalemate, third-world nationalism, and so on, China's policy toward the

United States would tend to be dictated by the need to prevent U.S.-Russian hegemony and collusion at the expense of China. For this reason, China would favor America's continued involvement in various parts of the world as a check on the growth of Soviet power and influence. China would thus continue a policy of avoiding overt clashes with the United States so long as the international environment is not seen as drastically changing.

The situation is obviously fluid, the more so if one takes into consideration China's internal politics which entered a new phase after the death of Chou En-lai in January 1976. It was quickly followed by the ascension of Hua Kuo-feng to power, the stripping of Teng Hsiao-p'ing of all his powers, the death of Mao Tse-tung, and attacks on "the gang of four," including Chiang Ch'ing, Mao's wife. One wonders where this will all end. Prognostication is extremely dangerous. As late as the summer of 1976 the China watchers were almost unanimous in discounting the possibility that Teng would ever end his days of disgrace, but these were the very people who had confidently asserted, before and shortly after Chou's death, that Teng would be his successor. At this writing there is a real possibility of Teng's restoration to a position of power, although one should be wary of discerning any clear pattern of personal and factional struggles in Chinese politics until at least a few years have passed.

But China as a state will face essentially identical challenges and opportunities, no matter who constitutes its temporary leadership. Among these challenges and opportunities will be the shifting power balances between the United States and the Soviet Union, persistent aspirations of the third world for a larger share of the globe's resources, efforts by the industrial democracies to cope with these aspirations in a framework of accommodation rather than confrontation, increasingly nationalistic definitions of fishery zones and air space, and the unsolved questions of the Middle East and Africa. The extent to which the power struggle between "the gang of four" and their opponents is related to a serious dispute on foreign policy will not be known for some time. It does seem possible that the "radicals" emphasize, because they thrive in, a crisis atmosphere which necessitates mass dedication to revolutionary zeal and justifies curtailment of internal freedom as well as external contact. In China they have tended to stress self-reliance in military and economic matters. The "moderates," by contrast, generally support a more balanced (i.e., traditional) approach to economic development, national security, and international affairs, accepting the need to turn to foreign capital and technology to supplement Chinese resources, and avoiding the hazard of antagonizing Russia and the United States simultaneously. Should they remain in power, therefore, they may seek a measure of equilibrium between the two superpowers. A precipitous American withdrawal from Asia, for instance, will almost certainly bring about a reassessment of China's relations with the Soviet Union. On the other hand, should the United States, under the new Carter Administration, stiffen its stand on the Taiwan and other questions, this may weaken the position of the "moderates" and strengthen more radical, purist, or isolationist forces in China, increasing the chances of the country moving into a sustained period of turmoil. Some of the "moderates" may argue for a favorable response to Soviet overtures for more "normal" relations, but less because they believe that any fundamental shift in Sino-Soviet relations is possible than to gain maneuverability and leverage vis-à-vis the United States. Moreover, if the Chinese leaders continue to de-emphasize certain domestic policies of Mao, their need for legitimacy will make it difficult substantially to modify his bitter animosity toward the Soviet Union.

[48]

In the final analysis, therefore, one has to ask if the Chinese leaders—whoever they turn out to be in the near future—prefer a more or less stable to a more or less turbulent world, including China. This is a matter of their perception of the whole international system, as the foregoing historical sketch indicates. To the extent that the Chinese leaders envision a stable international order, sustained by a power equilibrium around the globe, especially in Asia, their responses to external events will be along more predictable lines. They will stress peace and stability in the world so that they may concentrate on China's economic development. After Mao's death, the "moderates" have frequently invoked his call for "modernization" through the adoption of advanced technology. The Hua regime has also echoed Chou En-lai's insistence on "four modernization projects" (agriculture, industry, defense, and scientific technology). Of these four, the "moderates" not only in the Party but also in the army seem to have paid special attention to industrial modernization.[23] These instances may indicate an effort to minimize ideological aspects of Chinese policy and to visualize China as a developing nation, and lead to a greater desire for a stable relationship with the United States. If so, then there would be a degree of harmony of perception and of interests between Chinese and Americans, which could be expected to bring about deepened economic and cultural contacts. Because, in the late 1970s, the world stands at a threshold of an era where greater changes are likely to take place in economic and cultural, rather than in military and political, spheres of international affairs, such a development would be a welcome change from the story of power politics, misunderstanding, and wars that have characterized relations between China and the United States for most of their history.

NOTES

1. See Akira Iriye, "Continuities in U.S.-Japanese Relations, 1941-49," in Yōnosuke Nagai and Akira Iriye, eds., *Origins of the Cold War in Asia* (Tokyo: Tokyo University Press, and New York: Columbia University Press, 1977), pp. 378-407.

2. The most recent documentation on Chinese attitudes in 1945 can be found in Lyman Van Slyke, ed., *Marshall's Mission to China* (Arlington, Va.: University Publications of America, 1976).

3. Kennan memo, May 27, 1948, PPS 28/2, Joint Chiefs of Staff Papers, National Archives.

4. Joint Intelligence Staff memos, October 22 and 26, 1945, J.I.S. 80/5/M and 80/9, *ibid.*

5. Clark Clifford, "American Relations with the Soviet Union," September 24, 1946.

6. The best recent discussion of the subject is Tatsumi Okabe, "The Cold War and China," in Nagai and Iriye, *Origins,* pp. 224-51.

7. Cited in *ibid.,* p. 233.

8. See Nakajima Mineo, *Gendai Chūgoku to kokusai kankei* (Tokyo: Nihon Nōritsu Kyōkai, 1973), pp. 175-76.

9. NSC 76, July 21, 1950, JCS Papers.

10. For this view of the European Cold War, see D. C. Watt, "Britain and the Cold War in the Far East, 1945-58," in Nagai and Iriye, *Origins,* pp. 89-122.

11. Ōta Katsuhiro, *Mao Tse-tung gaikō rosen o kataru* (Tokyo: Gendai Hyōronsha, 1975), p. 114.

12. Robert R. Simmons, *The Strained Alliance: Peking, P'yongyang, Moscow and the Politics of the Korean Civil War* (New York: Free Press, 1975).

13. For a view that Peking's moves were prompted less by a desire for better relations with the United States than to undermine the Republic of China, see Richard Moorsteen and Morton Abramowitz, *Remaking China Policy: U.S.-China Relations and Government Decisionmaking,* (Cambridge, Mass., Harvard University Press, 1971), p. 4.

14. Mao's talks on September 5 and 8, 1958, published in *Mao Tse-tung ssu-hsiang wan-sui!* (n.p., 1969), reprinted in Ōta, pp. 45-61.

15. See Roderick MacFarquhar, *Sino-American Relations, 1949-71* (New York: Praeger Publishers, for the Royal Institute of International Affairs, 1972), esp. pp. 182-96, for a description of these developments.

16. See Nakamura Heiji, "Chū-In kankei no shodankai to sono kadai," in Irie Keishirō and Andō Seishi, eds., *Gendai Chūgoku no kokusai kankei* (Tokyo: Japan Institute of International Relations, 1975), pp. 377-407; and Allen Whiting, *The Chinese Calculus of Deterrence: India and Indo-China* (Ann Arbor: University of Michigan Press, 1975).

17. In *Jen-min Jih-pao,* May 21, 1970, printed in Ōta, pp. 131-33.

18. See, for example, the *Jen-min Jih-pao* editorial of January 21, 1964, as cited by Ōta Katsuhiro, "Chūgoku taigai seisaku no kiseki," in Irie and Andō, *Gendai Chūgoku,* p. 94.

19. See Nakajima, *ibid.,* p. 89.

20. Chou's talks with Japanese journalists, October 28, 1971, cited in Morishita Shūichi, *Chou En-lai: Chūgoku no naigai seisaku* (2 vols., Tokyo: Chūgoku Keizai Shinbunsha, 1973), I, pp. 891-98.

21. See, for instance, the documents cited in note 15, Chapter 6 in this book.

22. See A. Doak Barnett, "Peking and the Asian Power Balance," *Problems of Communism,* July-August 1976, pp. 36-48, for a good analysis of Chinese foreign policy choices involving balance-of-power considerations.

23. *Mainichi shinbun,* December 10, 1976.

[THREE]

Sino-American
Economic Relations *

Alexander Eckstein

Since the renewal of Sino-American contacts in 1969-70, trade and economic relations have served as a signaling device, ** a barometer, and a symbol rather than as a major motivating force for the normalization of relations between the two countries. From a negligible amount in 1971, Sino-American trade rose to a total turnover of $935 million in 1974, but declined to slightly less than half that amount in the following year. Furthermore, the interests of the two parties in trade and economic relations have been in part asymmetrical.

* The research on which this chapter is based was sponsored by The Brookings Institution. The author wishes to express his appreciation for their support and to make clear that the views expressed are his own.
** See Appendix, "Highlights of U.S.-China Trade."

[53]

There are some more or less serious institutional barriers to trade on our side. Yet once the embargo was lifted in mid-1971, we were anxious to move ahead as rapidly as possible within the legal constraints imposed by the Trade Act of 1974 and some other legal impediments and regulations.

In contrast, the Chinese were interested in the United States primarily as a residual supplier of farm products and, to a lesser extent, of certain types of equipment such as commercial jet aircraft, ammonia plants (for fertilizer production), and oil drilling equipment. Some of the barriers to trade could have been removed by bilateral agreements antedating formal diplomatic relations, but the Chinese backed off from these. From their vantage point, the state of commerce with the United States was necessarily viewed, at least in part, as a function of the state of political relations.

We wanted to promote trade and other types of exchanges as a means of building a momentum in the relationship, step by step, which would then gradually lead to normalization. In our view, this process could and would contribute to the rise of interest groups within the American business and scientific communities, which would press for speeding up normalization. However, the Chinese position has been that full normalization is a necessary precondition for advancing commercial and other exchanges.

With these political realities in mind, the evolution of Sino-American economic relations are explored in this chapter in the broader setting of China's economic development and foreign trade and its foreign trade policies. The effect of these on the level and composition of Chinese-American trade are examined, with particular emphasis on the interrelationships between economic and political variables. In conclusion, the outstanding policy issues affecting Sino-American economic relations and their prospects are analyzed.

[54]

The Role of Foreign Trade in China's Economic Development.

China's economic growth since 1949 has been very impressive by the country's past development standards and as compared with the pace of expansion of presently industrialized countries in the nineteenth century. It was also quite rapid, although not exceptional, in comparison with the postwar growth tempo of other underdeveloped countries.

Foreign trade has played a small but very significant role both in maintaining stability and in contributing to growth in China. Grain imports during the agricultural crisis of the early 1960s helped to alleviate food shortages and contain inflationary pressures, particularly in the cities. Imports of machinery, transport equipment, complete plants, and other capital goods fostered China's industrialization, modernization and technological progress and in this way contributed to China's economic growth.

The advantages derived from the international division of labor and specialization are more pronounced for small than for large countries, for the latter usually contain within their national boundaries varied and reasonably abundant natural resources. Moreover, large economies provide ample opportunity for regional specialization and an internal division of labor. Given the size of their markets, they can also take advantage of economies of scale within their national units. Therefore it is not surprising to find that, typically, the foreign trade of large countries is small in relation to their GNP, as compared to small countries. Thus foreign trade turnover (imports and exports combined) has been around 10 to 15 percent for the United States, less than 10 percent for India, and around 15 percent for Brazil, as compared to over 80

[55]

percent for the Netherlands, 30 to 40 percent for the United Kingdom, and about 20 percent for Japan. They were possibly around 6 percent for China and 5 to 6 percent for the Soviet Union.[1]

Of course these ratios are not constant from year to year, nor over longer periods. They reflect changes in economic structure, stages of development, and economic policy. In the Chinese case, it is quite clear that in the 1950s the economy was gradually becoming more oriented to foreign trade. This is evidenced by the fact that China's foreign trade turnover rose at an average annual rate of close to 14 percent between 1952 and 1959, while GNP grew at a 10 to 11 percent rate. The trend was reversed in the 1960s, with foreign trade turnover (in real terms) lagging considerably behind GNP. In the early 1970s, however, foreign trade once more began to expand quite rapidly. As a result, for the 1952-74 period as a whole it would seem that foreign trade rose only somewhat more slowly than the average annual GNP rate of about 6 percent.

Although foreign trade was relatively unimportant for the Chinese economy in aggregate terms, imports played a most significant role in structural and development terms. Imports of capital goods served as a major avenue for the transfer of advanced technology from abroad. During the 1950s these imports played a very large role in China's investment program, contributing about 40 percent to the equipment component of investment. These ratios declined significantly in the 1960s, but recovered somewhat in the 1970s. Thus the import component of investment in recent years may be around 10 percent.[2] It has been estimated that if China had completely cut itself off from imports between 1953 and 1957, the country's economic growth would have been reduced from an average annual rate of 6.5 percent to possibly 3 to 5 percent.[3] The data available at present are insufficient to make a similar estimate for the 1970s, but China's industrial progress over the past twenty years would make the cost of total autarky almost certainly substantially less. Import supplies also played an essential role in the provision of military matériel, particularly in the 1950s, and probably still do although to an unknown and probably smaller degree. In sharp contrast, food imports were quite unimportant in the 1950s, but acquired great significance in the next decade.

With the onset of an acute agricultural crisis between 1959 and 1962, China began to experience very severe shortages of food. Large-scale grain imports were initiated, at first on an emergency basis, which relieved the situation relatively easily and quickly. However, these imports, which at first contributed to China's economic and political stability, became a normal part of the country's food supply. They were particularly important in provisioning the cities and in building up and maintaining grain reserves. They served to ease the burden on the country's transport system and reduce the pressure on the peasantry to feed the cities. For instance, it may be simpler and less costly to ship grain from Vancouver to Shanghai than overland from the remote, surplus-producing province of Szechuan.

The importance of this trade is illustrated by the fact that during the depth of China's economic and agricultural crisis in 1961-62, food grain imports may have augmented domestic supplies available to the army and the urban population by about 30 to 40 percent, although they constituted less than 4 percent of total output.[4] In the 1970s the latter ratio was only about 1 to 2 percent, while the share of food grain imports in the urban food supply may at most constitute 10 percent.

Not only grain imports, but also machinery and equipment, metals, and chemical fertilizer have continued to be of crucial importance in China's economic development, particularly in the 1970s. Between 1970 and 1974, China imported about 35 million tons of fertilizer (in terms of gross weight); in nutrient content this provided one-quarter of China's total fertilizer supply. Although imported machinery and equipment played a much smaller role in total capital formation than in the 1950s, it was very important as a means of transferring advanced technology from abroad and thus accelerating China's technological progress in a wide range of categories, from electronics to petrochemicals. Its importance is also attested by the fact that in the 1970s one-fourth of China's total imports went into machinery and equipment; that is, about the same share as during the First Five Year Plan (FFYP) period (1953-57). In marked contrast, imports of metals, in particular specialty iron and steel products as well as nonferrous metals, rose greatly in importance from roughly less than 10 percent of China's purchases abroad in the FFYP period to about 25 percent in the 1970s.

THE FOREIGN TRADE POLICIES OF THE PEOPLE'S REPUBLIC OF CHINA

Since the founding of the People's Republic, China's foreign trade policies reflect a complex interaction between its foreign policies, its internal political developments, and the dictates of economic necessity or comparative advantage.

When China pursued a very active foreign trade policy in the 1950s, this orientation occurred within the context of a rather tightly knit Sino-Soviet alliance on the one hand and an ambitious industrialization program on the other. A policy directed toward maximizing the rate of industrial growth and building up China's defense establishment could at that time be implemented only by large-scale imports of capital goods and military matériel from the Soviet Union and Eastern Europe. The dependence was reinforced by the fact that strategic trade controls by the United States and its allies denied these products to China.

Thus economic and foreign policy combined to lead China into a preponderantly Soviet trade orientation. These policies not only shaped the direction of trade and its commodity composition, but also minimized the resistance to dependence on foreign trade itself. As Sino-Soviet tensions mounted there was some rising concern about China's preponderant dependence on a single trading partner, but there were no signs of animosity toward the import of foreign technology or the "worship of foreign things," nor were there any strong pressures for autarky at that time.

These attitudes changed radically, following the Sino-Soviet split of 1960. China's dependence on the Soviet Union was clearly evidenced by the fact that from 60 to 80 percent of its trade was with the Communist Bloc in the 1950s. During the same period the Soviet Union extended credits of $1.4 billion to $2.2 billion (depending on how these are estimated and converted from rubles and yuan into dollars), and sent about 11,000 Soviet specialists and technicians to China; to this number must be added another 1,500 technicians from Eastern Europe. The credits were phased out by 1957, and the technicians were withdrawn suddenly and abruptly in 1960 with attendant disruptions in Chinese industry, in some other sectors, and most notably in defense. The experience dramatized to the Chinese the high potential costs of dependence on any one country or any one source of supply.

This sharp turnabout happened to coincide with a profound agricultural and economic crisis in China, reflecting the far-reaching planning and technical errors during the Great Leap

Forward, which contributed to a series of very poor harvests. There is no doubt that the economic crisis was further aggravated by the sudden Soviet withdrawal. Thus the marked reduction in foreign trade between 1959 and 1962 (see Table 1) was a reflection of the depressed state of the Chinese economy that affected its import demand as well as its export capacity.

As the Chinese economy recovered from its deep depression, foreign trade was being restored as well, but at a slower pace than GNP. Thus while trade had led growth in the 1950s, it was lagging behind it in the 1960s. In part, this was due to the fact that a large number of complete plants imported in the late 1950s were still in the process of construction when the Soviet technicians suddenly left in 1960. Many were left standing uncompleted since even existing and completed installations were operating well below capacity at the time. As a result, there was no need to finish them until recovery was well under way in the mid-1960s.

The completion of these plants greatly expanded China's domestic capacity to produce machinery and a wide assortment of investment goods. Other things being equal, this in itself would have contributed to at least a temporary reduction in import demand. This tendency was reinforced, however, by a strong emphasis on self-reliance, buttressed by a series of major campaigns. At least initially, all this clearly represented a strong reaction to the Sino-Soviet break. Gradually the policy was broadened to encompass internal as well as external economic policy considerations and, as such, became firmly institutionalized.

Self-reliance never meant complete autarky but rather a deliberate pursuit of an import-substitution and import-minimization policy. The pursuit of this policy entailed at least some isolation of Chinese science, technology, and industry from the rest of the world in the 1960s. It also meant that China was cutting itself off from the world's capital markets and from access to even short- or medium-term commercial loans, not to speak of long-term credits. Under the impact of this policy, foreign purchases of machinery, transport equipment, and other capital goods were probably reduced to lower levels than might have prevailed otherwise.

To the extent that imports of capital goods serve as a major highway for the transfer of technology this policy must have been a factor in slowing down the rate of technological progress. At the same time, the posture of self-reliance left many enterprises to their own devices, forcing them to improvise or, to use the Chinese phrase, "take the initiative in their own hands." It meant, for instance, that if certain machinery components wore out they had to be replaced by domestically manufactured components. Necessarily it led to "learning by doing." Although initially this may have led to quite high costs and inefficient methods of production in many places, it almost certainly stimulated the rapid diffusion of production techniques already known and in process some- where within China, including those that were relatively advanced. Therefore it is difficult to assess whether on balance self-reliance retarded or accelerated technological progress.

The rhetoric and campaigns for self-reliance attained their height during the Cultural Revolution. As the active phase of the Cultural Revolution came to a halt in 1968-69 and normalcy gradually gained ground, Chinese policy makers began to weigh the costs of self-reliance against those of economic dependence on others. Out of this search for a new policy optimum there gradually crystallized a series of deci- sions, apparently made at the highest levels between 1970 and 1972, which involved a reinterpretation of the concept of self- reliance. It was apparently decided that China would once again pursue a more open foreign trade orientation and launch an active program of technological imports from abroad. At the same time, in order to minimize the vulnerabilities and risks of dependence, China would limit its reliance on any single source of supply and its overall financial or credit dependence on foreign countries.

Basically, this new line raises the priority ranking assigned to sustained and long-range economic development. It is evidenced by the new wave of economic expansion experienced in China since 1970, and by the large number of new projects launched since early 1972. The policy was most explicitly and authoritatively enunciated in the late Premier Chou En-lai's "Report on the Work of the Government," a speech delivered at the National People's Congress in January 1975, in which he sketched his hopes for China's future economic development. He spoke of turning "a poverty-striken and backward country into a socialist one *with the beginnings of prosperity in only twenty years and more.*" Before the end of the century, according to Premier Chou's program, China "is to *accomplish the comprehensive modernization of agriculture, industry, national defense and science and technology so that our national economy will be advancing in the front ranks of the world.*" [5]

From the standpoint of foreign economic policy, the key point is that the leadership seems to have recognized that the central elements in the new policy—increased investment, continued stress on rural development, including more fertilizer production and other agricultural assistance, and advanced technology generally—inevitably called for increased imports of capital goods and even some foreign credits. It was not possible to proceed very far along this road without coming into conflict with the more or less autarkic Chinese foreign trade policy that dominated the 1960s.

The shifts in trade and development policy were closely intertwined with foreign policy and security considerations, particularly the Chinese perceptions of a Soviet threat. It would seem that around 1970, Chairman Mao and Premier Chou decided to reformulate the Chinese strategy of coping with the Soviet threat. In the short run, the Chinese would seek reassurance against the threat by opening relations with the United States; in the longer run they would seek to build a "powerful, modern, socialist state."

Consequently, the self-reliance policy had to be reformulated. One of the most tangible signs of a policy shift was the reactivation of the Technical Export-Import Corporation in late 1972 and the very large number of orders placed by the Chinese for the importation of complete plants. It is estimated that the aggregate value of these turn-key contracts concluded between late 1972 and mid-1976 is around $3 billion.[6]

The new policy was also articulated explicitly in several publications, of which an article in the *People's Daily* of October 15, 1974, is one of the most significant. It states that

the basic principles of our socialist foreign trade are maintaining independence, keeping the initiative in our own hands, relying on our own efforts, achieving equality and mutual benefit, and each making up what the other lacks.... By advocating the principle of maintaining independence and keeping the initiative in our own hands, *we never mean that we advocate a policy of exclusion.* ... We have consistently held that *it is necessary to vigorously develop commerce and trade and carry out economic and technical exchanges with various countries and that these are necessary for and conducive to promoting the economic development of various countries* [emphasis added].

[63]

This was then further elaborated a few days later in a NCNA (New China News Agency) broadcast indicating that

> *China uses foreign trade to stimulate production, scientific research and internal trade.* . . . *China imports certain new techniques and industrial equipment in line with the principle of "making foreign things serve China."* This serves to reinforce the country's potentials of self-reliance and accelerate her socialist construction [emphasis added].[7]

But this policy shift encountered greater or lesser resistance all along from the ideological "left" who are strongly opposed to "worshipping foreign things." Thus several articles appeared in the *People's Daily* and in *Red Flag* attacking a more open foreign trade orientation during the anti-Lin and anti-Confucian campaign in 1974. Similar voices cropped up periodically during 1975.

The anti-foreign trade campaign gained in vigor and virulence with the death of Chou En-lai and the attendant purge of Teng Hsiao-p'ing. For example, the April 1976 issue of *Red Flag* carried an article entitled "Criticized the Slavish Compradore Philosophy," attacking that "unrepentant capitalist roader" who, it said, called last year for "pinning hope on foreign countries for the development of production and the development of science and technology"; at the same time he clamored for "bringing out more things to exchange for the latest and best foreign equipment." *Red Flag* then went on to argue that to exchange exports for imports in an unprincipled way would invariably lead to a situation where

> . . . we import everything that we can produce without restriction, export everything that is badly needed in the country without restriction, buy what is advanced from

others, produce what is backward ourselves, and *even give to others the sovereign right to open up mineral resources* [emphasis added]. Then as time passed, would we not turn our country into a market where the imperialist countries dump their goods, a raw material base, a repair and assembly workshop, and an investment center?

What has been the impact of these sharp controversies on actual trade policy and behavior? As noted above, the series of decisions made between 1970 and 1972 led to a greater involvement of China in the world economy. This is clearly illustrated by the very rapid growth in exports and imports—in terms of both current and constant prices—between 1970 and 1973. Why the slowing down in 1974 and 1975, as shown in Table 1?

Under the impact of a large new investment program in the Fourth Five Year Plan, the imports of machinery, equipment, and other producer goods were greatly stepped up, particularly in 1973. Moreover, due to an inferior harvest in 1972, imports of agricultural products—grain, cotton and soybeans—were stepped up markedly. Hence in 1973 there was a marked expansion in both industrial and agricultural imports at the same time. It was also the year that marked the height of the world economic boom so that China readily found markets for its expanding exports, thus earning the necessary foreign exchange with which to cover its growing import needs.

This situation was radically altered by the onset of a prolonged world *stagflation*. Given the development priorities set by the Fourth Five Year Plan, China continued its large investment program linked to the importation of complete plants and other types of investment goods. At the same time it was found necessary to continue agricultural imports at record levels. Amidst a raging world inflation all these products had to be imported at high world prices. At the same time in the face of a world recession, and an attendant decline in effective demand in most markets, China encountered great difficulties in placing its exports. As a result, imports expanded much faster than exports in 1974, thus producing China's largest trade deficit since 1949 of about one billion dollars.

The deficit necessarily required a curtailment in import orders as a means of narrowing the trade gap. This was evidenced by a very sharp reduction in the placement of new import contracts for complete plants and the stretch-out of grain shipments, both evident in the last quarter of 1974. The policy was continued in 1975 so that exports and imports rose very little in terms of current prices and almost certainly declined in real quantum terms.

There has been a great deal of speculation that the slowing down and virtual halt in new complete plant contracts reflected a shift back to a more autarkic trade policy under the pressure of the anti-Confucian campaign and the attacks on foreign trade dependence cited above; and that the same reasons explain the general slow-down in China's trade in the last year or two. While this possibility cannot be ruled out, as I tried to show above, recent foreign trade trends seem to reflect an interaction between China's internal development requirements and world economic trends rather than a shift in trade policy back in an autarkic direction.

This conclusion is buttressed by the fact that even amidst these vituperative attacks on foreign trade, even in the early months of 1976, both high-ranking and working-level officials of the Foreign Trade Ministry and of the Ministry of Foreign Affairs have repeatedly gone out of their way to reassure visiting foreign statesmen as well as businessmen that China plans to continue an active import and export program without any marked shifts in overall trade policy. Of course this does not mean that the possibility of a shift can be eliminated, but merely that thus far the anti-trade opposition does not seem to have prevailed. At the same time, it is not entirely clear how seriously or literally these attacks were meant. They were often full of ambiguities and contradictions; moreover they must be interpreted as part and parcel of a much broader political struggle for the succession to Chou and Mao in which a great deal of exaggerated rhetoric was used to attack Teng Hsiao-p'ing and other opponents. In any case, it would seem that the anti-trade opposition was dealt a severe blow by the purge of the so-called radicals in the late months of 1976.

Irrespective of these controversies, it is striking that Chinese statements concerning trade policy and potential gains from trade seem to place primary stress on the role of imports rather than exports. This is in contrast to conventional approaches to foreign trade, which place the emphasis on the role of exports and export-led growth.

The Chinese attitude is in part a reflection of the fact that, in general, centrally planned command economies tend to have a pronounced autarkic bias. Therefore foreign trade policy controversies revolve around the margin; that is, not around questions of "either-or," but rather "how much more or less." This bias is motivated by several types of considerations. Trends in the world economy are much more difficult to forecast than at home; therefore involvement in the international economy adds an element of uncertainty and unpredictability, which is necessarily disconcerting from a planner's point of view. Moreover, enterprises in such a system are not aggressively oriented to sales- and profit-maximization; they produce for the plan, based on certain targets, with outlets for their products guaranteed. Thus they have no incentive to seek markets for their products abroad. In essence, they are supply- rather than demand-oriented.

The tendency is strongly reinforced by the sharp separation

of producers and traders in China and in many other command economies. That is, producing enterprises are not involved in foreign trade. They rarely deal directly with foreign buyers or sellers. Rather they deal with foreign trade corporations which have a sole export-import monopoly in a broad product line (e.g., cereals, machinery, etc.) The whole marketing burden falls on these corporations rather than on the producing enterprises.

The planner charged with maximizing the rate of economic growth or some alternative economic goal articulates and elaborates the production or other plans. In the process he discovers certain shortages in raw material supplies either because certain minerals or other natural resources are not found within the country's boundaries, are not available in the requisite quantities, or are obtainable only at unusually high costs of extraction and/or transport. At the same time, for output to grow as production ceilings are reached with existing plant capacity, the pressures mount for new investment, for expanding plant and equipment. In developing economies many types of machinery and equipment either cannot be produced at home or can only be produced with great difficulty, at high cost and poor quality. The more complex and technologically advanced such machinery is, the more probable that it will have to be imported from abroad.

In addition, imports can alleviate certain rigidities in the planning process. As certain anticipated and particularly unanticipated shortages or production bottlenecks develop, they can often be more quickly and easily removed—and with less disruptive consequences for the planning process—by imports than by reallocations of domestic supplies. Therefore imports may play a crucial role in supplying raw material and food, in alleviating short-term bottlenecks, in supplying some major investment components, and in serving as the highway for the importation of technology. Imported technology is of critical importance in pacing the rate of technological progress in the developing country, both in its embodied form as machinery and in its disembodied form as know-how, blueprints, and other kinds of technical information.

In this type of economic system, under the conditions of an underdeveloped and continental economy, and for all the reasons cited above, the motivating force for foreign trade comes from the import rather than export side. The need to import provides the inducement to search for export supplies and export surpluses in order to finance imports. This seems to have characterized the approach of Soviet planners earlier and of Chinese planners since their First Five Year Plan (1953-57).

The Evolution of China's Foreign Trade

As one surveys the evolution of China's foreign trade since 1952 (used as a reference year because by then the Chinese economy had recovered from war devastation), several key characteristics stand out. Trade grew very rapidly between 1952 and 1959; that is, until the onset of the agricultural crisis. Comparatively, China's trade expanded much faster than total world trade, trade of all underdeveloped countries, or trade of all Asian countries as a group. After 1959, trade declined, recovered, then declined again, and finally increased once more in the 1970s. Under the impact of this fluctuating pattern, total trade turnover adjusted for price changes remained below the peak 1959 levels right up to 1972 (see Table 1). In brief, foreign trade stagnated in the 1960s and only in 1973 did it rise very significantly.

[69]

TABLE 1

China's Foreign Trade, Selected Years, 1952-75
(in millions of U.S. dollars)

Year	In Current Prices			In Constant 1963 Prices		
	Exports	Imports	Total Turnover	Exports	Imports	Total Turnover
1952	875	1,015	1,890	795	1,005	1,800
1955	1,375	1,660	3,035	1,295	1,715	3,010
1959	2,230	2,060	4,290	2,315	2,085	4,400
1961	1,525	1,490	3,015	1,540	1,520	3,060
1962	1,525	1,150	2,675	1,585	1,180	2,765
1966	2,210	2,035	4,245	2,155	1,915	4,070
1967	1,945	1,950	3,895	1,930	1,840	3,770
1968	1,945	1,820	3,765	1,920	1,735	3,655
1969	2,030	1,830	3,860	1,920	1,690	3,610
1970	2,050	2,240	4,290	1,865	1,890	3,755
1971	2,415	2,305	4,720	2,180	1,880	4,060
1972	3,085	2,835	5,920	2,570	2,115	4,685
1973	4,960	5,130	10,090	3,039	2,847	5,886
1974	6,515	7,490	14,005	2,856	3,200	6,056
1975	6,930	7,385	14,315	NA	NA	NA

Sources: Current price series from N.R. Chen, "China's Foreign Trade, 1950-74," in *China: A Reassessment of the Economy,* a Compendium of Papers Submitted to the Joint Economic Committee, 94th Congress, 1st Session, July 10, 1975, p. 645. Constant price data based on deflators derived by A. Eckstein in "China's Economic Growth and Foreign Trade," in *U.S.-China Business Review,* Vol. 1, No. 4 (July-August 1974). For 1973 and 1974, trade data in current prices obtained from CIA, Research Aid, *People's Republic of China, International Trade Handbook* (Washington, D.C., October 1975), p. 9; these were converted into 1963 prices for 1973 and 1974 on the basis of deflators derived by N.R. Chen in the article cited above. 1975 data in current prices obtained from CIA, Research Aid, *People's Republic of China, Handbook of Economic Indicators* (Washington, D.C. August 1976), p. 33.

China's trade was characterized not only by sharp fluctuations in volume but by marked shifts in direction, reflecting major turning points in China's foreign relations. As may be seen from Table 2, the preponderant bulk of the country's foreign trade was with the Soviet Bloc in the 1950s. In large part this was in response to Mao's "lean-to-one-side" policy enunciated upon the founding of the People's Republic. However, this tendency was reinforced by the facts that the United States imposed a total embargo on all trade and payments with China and that most other countries participated in a system of more or less tight controls on the shipment to the People's Republic of a wide variety of goods that were considered strategic. In short, China's preponderant pro-Soviet trade orientation in the 1950s was in part a matter of choice and in part imposed by necessity.

This situation was greatly altered by the Sino-Soviet break in 1960 and the gradual relaxation of controls on trade with China by most countries, except the United States. As a result, we see a complete reversal: while 70 to 80 percent of China's trade was with the Bloc in the 1950s and only 20 to 30 percent with the non-Communist world, the ratios were reversed in the 1960s. Japan and Hong Kong became China's leading trading partners, while both the Soviet Union and Eastern Europe greatly declined in importance. At the same time, China's trade with Asian Communist countries (North Vietnam and North Korea in particular)—ranged in Table 2 under "other socialist countries"—made great gains.

The process of trade reorientation continued in the 1970s, marked especially by a further decline in the relative importance of the Soviet Union. This process reached its nadir in 1970, when, following the Chenpao (Damyanski) Island border clash of 1969, Sino-Soviet relations reached their low

TABLE 2

Direction of China's Foreign Trade in Selected Years[a]
(in percent)

	1955		1965		1975	
	Exports	Imports	Exports	Imports	Exports	Imports
Socialist Countries	70	78	32	28	20	13
of which:						
Soviet Union	48	57	11	10	2	2
Eastern Europe	17	18	7	7	7[c]	7[c]
Other[b]	5	3	14	11	11[c]	4[c]
Non-Socialist Countries	30	22	68	72	80	87
of which:						
Japan	6	2	11	14	21	32
Hongkong	11	2	17	negl.	15	negl.
Western Europe	8	7	15	19	12	27
United States	—	—	—	—	2	5
Other	5	13	25	38	30	23
Total	100	100	100	100	100	100

[a] All percentages are rounded to the nearest number.

[b] Includes Asian Communist countries, Cuba and Yugoslavia.

[c] These percentages are not fully comparable with those for earlier years, since Albania is included under Eastern Europe in 1955 and 1965, but is ranged under other Communist countries in 1974; as a result, the 1974 figures understate the share of Eastern Europe and correspondingly overstate it for the other Communist states.

Sources: A. Eckstein, *Communist China's Economic Growth and Foreign Trade* (New York, 1966), Table 4-3, p. 98; R. Dernberger, "Prospects for Trade Between China and the United States," in A. Eckstein, *China Trade Prospects and U.S. Policy* (New York, 1971), Appendix Table A3, pp. 280-97; Joint Economic Committee, Congress of the United States, *People's Republic of China, An Economic Assessment* (Washington, D.C., May 18, 1972), Table 10, pp. 350-51; CIA, Research Aid, *People's Republic of China, International Trade Handbook,* Washington, D.C., October 1976), Table 4, p. 15.

point. That year only about 1 percent of China's trade was with the Soviets, with a modest recovery since then. At the same time Japan strengthened its position as China's leading trading partner, and an important new element was introduced: the rise of the United States as a major trading partner. As will be shown in greater detail in the next section, the United States occupied a very significant place in China's trade in 1973 and 1974. However, by 1975 only 5 percent of China's imports came from the United States (instead of 13 percent in the preceding year), while China's export share to the United States remained at around 2 percent.

Fluctuations in volume and shifts in the direction of trade were paralleled by significant changes in the commodity composition of exports and imports. In large part, these changes reflected the marked structural transformation experienced by the Chinese economy, with agriculture's share of GNP diminishing while industry's weight was rising rapidly. This, combined with a deliberate import-substitution policy, had a profound impact on the character of import demand and the availability of export supplies, as illustrated by the data in Tables 3A and 3B.

The much more highly industrialized state of the economy, reinforced by the policy of self-reliance, is most clearly reflected in the fact that the importance of machinery and equipment imports declined, as compared both to total imports and to domestic production. At the same time, imports of semi-manufactured metals were rising rapidly in the 1960s, both in absolute and relative terms. These were mostly high quality iron and steel materials and nonferrous metals used in the production of machinery and military end-items. China was, in effect, reducing its import dependence in this way by substituting the relatively less costly semi-manufactures for imported end-items in the capital goods industries.

TABLE 3A

Commodity Composition of China's Imports, 1955-73[a]
(in percent)

Commodity Category	1955	1959	1966	1970	1973
1. Food, Beverages and Tobacco	2.2	0.3	27.1	19.2	18.7
2. Crude Materials, inedible	11.1	13.4	16.4	11.3	17.8
of which, textile fibers	(8.0)	(5.6)	(7.1)	(5.4)	(9.5)
3. Mineral Fuels and Lubricants	7.4	6.5	0.2	0.2	0.1
4. Animal and Vegetable Oils and Fats	0.5	0.2	0.2	0.3	1.0
5. Chemicals	9.6	8.1	12.6	15.5	10.0
of which chemical fertilizer	(3.7)	(2.5)	(7.1)	(7.5)	(4.3)
6. Manufactured Goods, by material	12.4	17.9	18.7	33.3	31.0
of which metals and metals manufactures	(8.9)	(15.4)	(16.2)	(29.1)	(28.2)
7. Machinery and Transport Equipment	22.4	40.0	19.1	15.1	15.6
8. Miscellaneous Manufactures	2.6	2.2	2.4	1.3	1.1
9. Goods Not Elsewhere Specified	31.8	11.4	3.3	3.4	4.7

[a] Figures in parentheses represent subcategories.

Sources: These percentages were derived by the author from annual commodity composition data published by the U.S. Department of Commerce for non-Communist World trade in annual *Reports to Congress* by the U.S. Mutual Defense Assistance Control Administrator; these were combined with Soviet data for their trade with China published in *The Foreign Trade of the USSR, Statistical Handbook* for various years. Non-Communist world and Soviet trade combined accounted for 79 to 88 percent of China's total imports between 1952 and 1973.

While the importance of capital goods declined, that of foods, particularly grains, rose very markedly. In the 1950s China exported between 500,000 and 1,600,000 tons of rice and imported virtually no grains at all. Both in quantity and value, China was a significant net grain exporter. That position was drastically reversed beginning in 1961 when

China imported over 6 million tons of grain, mostly wheat, and has continued these imports ever since in varying quantities, depending on the state of the harvest in China. In the meantime, rice exports shrunk under the impact of the crisis in the early 1960s but then gradually recovered and even exceeded their former peak levels.[8] The energy food value of rice and wheat are roughly equivalent. Since the world price of a ton of rice is appreciably higher than that of a ton of wheat, China could obtain a net foreign exchange gain by exporting rice and importing wheat. Yet since 1961 and up to 1973 it would seem that rice exports consistently lagged behind other grain imports in terms of both tonnage and value.

TABLE 3B

Commodity Composition of China's Exports, 1955-73[a]
(in percent)

Commodity Category	1955	1959	1966	1970	1973
1. Food, Beverages and Tobacco	32.8	26.2	30.8	29.1	25.2
2. Crude Materials, inedible	36.9	24.4	18.7	18.6	17.6
of which, textile fibers	(8.0)	(7.2)	(4.6)	(5.7)	(8.5)
3. Mineral Fuels and Lubricants	0.6	0.4	0.9	0.5	1.3
4. Animal and Vegetable Oils and Fats	3.5	1.3	1.9	1.0	0.6
5. Chemicals	2.1	2.6	3.3	5.0	4.8
6. Manufactured Goods, by material	18.3	25.8	20.4	25.8	25.6
of which: textiles	(8.8)	(18.1)	(11.6)	(17.7)	(15.7)
metals and metals manufactures	(7.9)	(5.0)	(4.8)	(3.2)	(4.4)
7. Machinery and Transport Equipment	1.1	1.5	1.2	2.6	2.3
8. Miscellaneous Manufactures	1.8	12.9	7.9	9.2	13.3
9. Other	2.9	4.9	14.9	8.2	9.3

[a] Figures in parentheses represent subcategories.

Sources: Same as for Table 3A.

Other significant changes in the commodity composition of China's trade involve chemical fertilizers and petroleum and its products. In the 1950s China imported chemical fertilizer in rather small quantities, well below 1 million metric tons. As China sharply redirected its development strategy around 1961 under the impact of its agricultural and economic crisis, a much higher priority in the allocation of resources was assigned to agriculture and the development of those industries which support agriculture by supplying its production requisites. This then led to a very rapid expansion of domestic fertilizer production capacity, and a stepping-up of fertilizer imports from about 1 million tons in the early 1960s to more than 7 million tons in the early 1970s.

The opposite happened in the case of petroleum and its products. For a long time it was thought that China was poorly endowed with oil resources. Domestic production was small and China was quite dependent on imported petroleum supplies, as evidenced by the fact that about a quarter of crude oil requirements and well over half of domestic gasoline, kerosene, and diesel oil needs had to be met through imports in the mid-1950s. In face of the strategic trade controls prevailing at the time, China could obtain petroleum products only from Russia and Romania. With the Sino-Soviet break, the People's Republic was determined to emancipate itself from any dependence on foreign oil.

An active program of geological exploration was launched, and as a result several major oil-producing fields were discovered in the late 1960s. Moreover, United Nations surveys found geological structures indicating that large offshore oil deposits might be found on the continental shelf. With the exploitation of the new fields in the Northeast and North, oil production has been rising very rapidly, at an average annual rate of about 20 to 30 percent since the early

1960s. Consequently China, which spent about 10 percent of its export earnings for the purchase of oil and its products in the 1950s, is on the way to becoming a significant exporter of petroleum in the 1970s.

Corresponding shifts are visible in other imports and exports. Thus agricultural products (both foodstuffs and raw materials) which dominated China's exports in the 1950s, diminished in importance and were in part replaced by manufactures in the 1960s and early 1970s. A major reason for the decline in food exports has been the steady erosion of soybean and oilseed surpluses, which contributed close to 20 percent of China's export supplies in the mid-1950s. China exported about 1 million or more tons of soybeans in the late 1950s. Shipments shrunk drastically during the agricultural depression years and, although they turned up again in the mid-1960s, never recovered. On the contrary, they declined more or less continuously to the point that net soybean exports in 1973 dwindled to 37,000 tons. Since then the PRC's soybean trade position has been shifting year by year. In 1974 it was a net importer, in 1975 a small net exporter, and it seems that in 1976 it may revert to a small net import situation.

The declines in agricultural products were more than offset by the increasing role of textiles—yarn, fabrics and clothing. Textile exports were sustained at high levels throughout the agricultural crisis years (1960-62) and played a crucial role at the time in supplying the foreign exchange earnings required to finance China's grain purchases abroad. Textile shipments remained at a high level even when the country's total imports were shrinking. This high level of textile exports could be maintained through the depression years only by cutting domestic textile rations to the bare bone. But significantly, these rations were greatly liberalized as China's economic situation improved. As textile production recovered and expanded, most of the increase in output apparently went into domestic consumption rather than exports. Consequently, the volume of textile exports adjusted for price changes was in 1973 probably not significantly above the earlier peak 1959 levels or much above the levels of the mid-1960s.

Another category of goods which exhibited a steady export rise is manufactured consumer goods such as watches, ball point pens, thermos bottles, furniture, as well as some durables like bicycles. These grew in absolute terms as well as in relation to total exports.

SINO-AMERICAN TRADE RELATIONS

Contrary to all earlier forecasts and projections, China's trade with the United States rose dramatically between 1971 and 1974. Once the trade embargo was lifted by the United States in mid-1971 and the Shanghai Communiqué defined the character of the relationship between the two countries some months thereafter, the major barriers to Sino-American trade relations were removed; in fact, their removal proceeded much more rapidly than had been anticipated.

A second factor which propelled Sino-American trade beyond projected levels was China's willingness to tolerate a highly imbalanced trade, as may be seen from Table 4. It was generally assumed that two-way trade would more or less have to be in balance and therefore, to the extent that the American market for Chinese goods might be quite limited, this would limit not only U.S. imports, but U.S. exports as well. But this did not turn out to be the case.

Probably the most crucial factor propelling U.S.-China trade was the coincidence in time of the opening of relations and a poor harvest in China. Until 1972, China purchased its grain—principally wheat—from Canada and Australia and, on occasion, smaller quantities from Argentina and France. However, with China increasing its grain imports by more than 50 percent between 1972 and 1973-74, Australia and Canada could not supply the large additional quantities, particularly in a tight world grain market. Thus of the 7.7 million tons delivered in 1973, about 4 million came from the United States, over 2 million from Canada, and close to 1 million from Australia. In 1974 close to 3 million tons were shipped from the United States, about 2 million from Canada, 1.5 million from Australia, and smaller amounts from Argentina and France.

TABLE 4

U.S. Trade with the People's Republic of China, 1971-76
(in millions of U.S. dollars)

Year	Exports	Imports
1971	Negl.	5.0
1972	63.5	32.4
1973	740.2	64.0
1974	820.5	114.7
1975	303.6	158.3
1976[a]	135.0	201.0

[a] (Editor's addendum.)

Sources: For 1971 to 1974: William Clarke and Martha Avery, "The Sino-American Commercial Relationship," in *China, A Reassessment of the Economy,* A Compendium of Papers Submitted to the Joint Economic Committee, 94th Congress, 1st Session, July 10, 1975, p. 512. For 1975: U.S. Department of Commerce, Bureau of East-West Trade, *U.S. Trade Status with Socialist Countries,* June 15, 1976, p. 2. For 1976: CIA, Office of Economic Research.

[79]

Following the inferior 1972 harvest, China stepped up its other agricultural purchases as well, particularly—as noted before—soybeans and cotton. These too could most readily be obtained in the United States, thus driving up further our exports to China. It is not surprising therefore that over 80 percent of American exports to China have been agricultural and less than 20 percent consisted of industrial and transport equipment and other manufactures in 1973 and 1974, as shown in Table 5A. But this commodity composition was also contrary to earlier expectations when it was generally assumed that if and when trade opened up, the United States would become a major capital goods supplier to China. Instead, Japan has played this role since the 1960s.

The originally expected pattern was more closely approximated in 1975 when U.S. exports to China were sharply curtailed. In late 1974 the Chinese began to reduce the quantities of farm products they ordered, while deliveries on contracts already firmed up were being stretched out. In large part this was due to a succession of two good harvests in 1973 and 1974. But the sharp curtailment of agricultural imports from the United States was also prompted by the fact that much of the wheat delivered by us to China was full of impurities, while the corn was so high in moisture content that some of it arrived sprouting. Under these conditions China naturally looked first to its traditional sources of supply, Australia and Canada, with which the PRC had long-term grain delivery contracts in any case. The United States was therefore in effect cast in the role of a residual supplier.

As a result of this drop in our exports, the U.S.-China trade imbalance was markedly narrowed from ratios of about 11:1 in 1973 and 8:1 in 1974 to approximately 2:1 in 1975. This reflects a marked reduction in agricultural shipments on the one hand and some continued growth in our imports from China on the other. Moreover, the commodity composition of our exports is changing markedly. In 1975, wheat and other grains disappeared entirely from our export shipments to China. Raw cotton maintained its relative position, but declined sharply in quantity and value. At the same time, there was some expansion in the sale of machinery and equipment, as well as of some industrial materials such as aluminum and alloys and fabricated steel. Consequently our exports to the PRC are no longer preponderantly agricultural.

This analysis clearly suggests that the dynamic factor in U.S.-China trade has been the Chinese demand for our products. Fluctuations in this demand are producing sharp fluctuations in total trade turnover. As a result, our trade with China moved from a negligible level in 1971 to eleventh place in 1972, only to rise to second place by 1973 and 1974 and then slip to fifth place in 1975. In marked contrast, U.S.

TABLE 5A

Commodity Composition of U.S. Exports to China, 1973-74
(in percent)

Commodity Category	1973	1974
Wheat	41.5	28.6
Corn	19.1	11.7
Cotton	13.6	22.7
Aircraft and parts	8.4	9.3
Soybeans	7.5	16.9
Iron and steel scrap	3.3	1.6
Fertilizer	0.6	negl.
Telecommunication equipment	0.6	0.1
Other	5.4	9.2

Source: William Clarke and Martha Avery, "The Sino-American Commercial Relationship," in *China, A Reassessment of the Economy,* a Compendium of Papers Submitted to the Joint Economic Committee, 94th Congress, 1st Session, July 10, 1975, Table 4, p. 513.

TABLE 5B

Commodity Composition of U.S. Imports from China, 1973-74
(in percent)

Commodity Category	1973	1974
Tin	12.0	8.2
Bristles, feathers and down	10.5	6.9
Cotton fabrics	10.3	22.3
Works of art, antiques	8.6	6.8
Raw silk	6.8	2.4
Pyrotechnical products	4.9	1.0
Rosin	8.6	6.8
Clothing and other textile products	3.1	6.0
Essential oils	2.3	4.2
Wood and resin-based chemicals	2.4	6.0
Wool and other animal hair	2.8	1.7
Fish and shellfish	1.5	6.2
Tobacco	1.5	2.3
Other	24.7	19.2

Source: Same as Table 5A, Table 5, p. 514.

imports from China have been much more stable and have risen continuously though quite slowly. In effect, the earlier projections concerning the market prospects for Chinese products in the United States have turned out to be fairly valid. Thus, American imports from China comprise cotton textiles, raw materials, such as tin, raw silk and silk products, and a variety of minor consumer items and some luxury products, as illustrated in Table 5B. As none of these imports can count on large mass markets in the United States, the opportunities for a dramatic expansion of Chinese sales are necessarily limited.

The limiting factors in Sino-American trade have been two: the market for China's products in the United States and

China's capacity to sustain a large and continuing deficit in its trade with us. China's ability to sell in the United States is in turn constrained by the country's total export level but, more importantly, by the limited market here for its products. For instance, one of China's major exports has been textiles. Other Asian countries, notably Taiwan, Hong Kong, Singapore, and Korea are competing for sales in a protected American market. Moreover, the Chinese are handicapped in this competition by virtue of the fact that their products have to bear the burden of the full U.S. tariff, while most of the other countries are subject to MFN (most favored nation) treatment.

Several attempts have been made to estimate the potential impact of MFN treatment on Chinese exports to the U.S. Unfortunately these studies, based on widely varying assumptions and methodologies, arrive at sharply differing results. According to one, the MFN impact would be rather modest, with U.S. imports from China rising by an estimated 16 percent.[9] An entirely different approach based on the assumption of full normalization of relations in all respects—i.e., full diplomatic recognition, settlement of the private claims and assets problem, granting of MFN treatment, and removal of all other trade barriers—concludes that our purchases from the PRC might be trebled or quadrupled.[10] A new and more systematic study of this problem is under way at present, but its results will not become available for some time.

In light of all these considerations, one can certainly conclude that granting of MFN would increase Chinese exports to the U.S., but by an unknown amount. On the one hand, it would increase the quantities of products already being sold; and on the other, it would open the way to new products (such as fabrics and garments of man-made fibres, shoes, paper products, electronic and electrical products), which cannot now compete in the U.S. market. At the same time it must be recognized that at least in the short run Chinese export supplies tend to be quite inelastic so that substantial increases in sales to the United States would require diversion from other markets. This could still contribute to an increase in China's export earnings if prices in American markets were higher than elsewhere.

Nevertheless, there is no doubt that even in the face of existing trade barriers (including MFN), Chinese exports to the United States could be increased with additional effort by all concerned. This would require aggressive salesmanship by the Chinese, extensive advertising of their products, and some further accommodation by China's trading corporations to the requirements of the American market. For instance, they may need to show greater readiness to grant special trademarks to large quantity buyers and adapt to certain special styling and labeling requirements. Some progress along these lines has already been made as Chinese trading officials have come into increasing contact with American businessmen at the Canton fair and elsewhere. The process has also been facilitated by the visits to the United States of Chinese trading delegations in certain special fields such as textiles, minerals and metals, and several others.

Expanding the market for Chinese products in the United States would not only represent a commercial gain for the PRC but could also greatly contribute to raising the exports of our products to China. Trade does not need to be balanced; but the smaller the deficit, the less the strain on China's balance of payments and the greater the inducement—other things being equal—for the Chinese to buy in the United States. Thus it is in the interests of certain American exporters to promote Chinese sales in our markets. This had been recognized by the Japanese some time ago, and through the extensive activities of the National Council for United States-China Trade this is beginning to be understood by some American businessmen as well.

Realistically, all these efforts combined can be expected to yield at best only modest increases in Chinese sales in the United States. Therefore if trade is to be balanced, or even if the imbalance is not to exceed a 2:1 ratio, American exports to China will necessarily be limited unless the PRC were to find means for financing the trade deficit. China maintains a sizable surplus in its trade with Hong Kong and Southeast Asia. In recent years the PRC has also obtained one or another form of banking credit in Japan and Western Europe. Thus the foreign exchange earned through a combination of these means can be applied to covering deficits in Sino-American trade, which is precisely what happened in 1973 and 1974. But China incurs deficits also in its trade with Japan, and in recent years with Western Europe as well. Necessarily then, this limits its capacity to finance trade deficits with the United States.

The balance-of-payment constraints were particularly pronounced in 1974 when the PRC incurred a record trade deficit of about $1 billion, followed by another deficit of about $400 million in 1975. This necessarily influenced China's ability and willingness to continue to finance a large trade deficit with the United States. These balance-of-payment constraints limiting the expansion of United States exports to China could be alleviated or removed in either one of two ways: through sizable oil shipments from China to the United States and/or United States credits to China. The possibilities are explored at greater length below.

Unresolved Policy Issues in Sino-American Relations

There are a number of remaining barriers to the growth of Sino-American trade in addition to those already touched upon. Possibly the most important revolves around barriers to financing Sino-American trade. The Jackson-Vanik amendment of the Trade Act of 1974 bars the extension of government or government-backed credits to countries that limit emigration, and these provisions seem to apply to China as well to the Soviet Union. Irrespective of the Trade Act, our Export-Import Bank could extend credits to China only if there were a Presidential determination that this would be in the national interest, since such determination is required for all such credits to Communist countries. Finally, according to Ex-Im Bank regulations, new credits cannot be extended to countries that have debts outstanding with the Bank. In this case, such debts were incurred by the Nationalist Government before 1949. This then becomes entangled in the issue of public claims against China and whether the PRC is willing to recognize obligations incurred by preceding regimes.

At the same time, private bank credits to China are complicated by the private claims-frozen assets problem. The U.S. Foreign Claims Settlement Commission awarded a total of about $176.4 million in private claims against the PRC. In turn, during the Korean War the United States blocked Chinese dollar assets in the United States valued at approximately $76.5 million.[11] Both figures refer to principal, exclusive of accumulated interest. Until this issue is resolved, direct banking relations between the two countries are precluded since any new Chinese assets (e.g., bank deposits) and commodities could be attached by private claimants in the United States. For this same reason, it would be difficult to mount Chinese trade exhibits in the United States.

Not all of these barriers present equally serious obstacles to Sino-American economic relations. Almost certainly the Jackson-Vanik amendment is the most restrictive. It bars credit and MFN treatment and is not negotiable; it can only be modified by legislative action. In contrast, virtually all the other institutional barriers could be removed by intergovernmental agreements. MFN treatment is also barred by virtue of the fact that the Trade Act of 1974 mandates that MFN can only be granted within the context of an intergovernmental trade agreement. The absence of direct banking relations is a less serious problem since all transactions can be carried out through subsidiaries of American banks abroad or through third-country banks.

There are absolutely no indications that the Chinese would be prepared to conclude a trade agreement with the United States short of diplomatic recognition. It would also seem that they are not interested in settling the private claims-frozen assets problem until full normalization is attained. Apparently all of the key issues concerning private claims and assets were resolved at least two years ago with a settlement based on an "even-steven" approach. However, the Chinese have held up consummation of this agreement, apparently tying it to formal recognition. This position was again reaffirmed recently by the Vice-Minister of Foreign Trade in an interview with an American delegation of foreign affairs specialists. Yet, some international banking and trading sources reported in the fall of 1976 that the private claims-frozen assets problem may be resolved some time after the American elections.[12]

These obstacles to the development of fully normalized trade relations have placed American exporters of machinery, equipment, and all types of capital goods at a competitive disadvantage in the China market. Our exports to China of all types of industrial goods, including machinery and transport equipment, were about $90 million in 1973, $140 million in

1974, and perhaps around $150 million in 1975. During these years, China's imports of these types of goods averaged from around $3 billion to $3.5 billion. Thus the United States supplied only 3 to 5 percent of China's imports of industrial goods, with Japan assuming by far the leading role. The cost advantages of Japanese industry are reinforced by Japan's geographic and cultural proximity to China. Furthermore, Japan has formal diplomatic relations with the People's Republic while we do not. Another very significant factor in this equation is that Japanese corporations and industrial firms are in a position to provide financing of the Export-Import Bank type for the sale of complete plants. This has greatly facilitated such sales to China, usually on five-year credit at concessionary interest rates and with repayments starting when the new facility becomes operational.

To this list of barriers standing in the way of unfettered trade relations with the PRC one must add export controls, which in some ways represent one of the most vexing and complex problems for the United States both in terms of policy and day-to-day administration. The policy guiding export controls and its administration cannot be divorced from the broad strategic outlook and posture of the United States not only vis-à-vis China but the Soviet Union as well. One of the fundamental issues in this context is whether our policy should be based on the principle of "evenhandedness" in terms of our treatment of China and the Soviet Union or should we "tilt" toward China.

It could be, and it has been, argued that it would be in our national interest to strengthen China's defense and deterrent capabilities in relation to the Soviet Union as part and parcel of maintaining a strategic balance.[13] More specifically, it is certainly in our interest to keep Soviet forces presently deployed in Asia (an estimated one-quarter of Russia's armed strength) from being transferred to Europe. However, in pursuing this policy we would not wish to exacerbate Sino-Soviet tensions to the point of risking an armed conflict between them, nor would we, as a result of this policy, want to increase tensions between the United States and the Soviet Union to the point of seriously jeopardizing our bilateral relations, arms control negotiations with the Russians, or driving them into retaliatory action against us in other parts of the world. This then necessarily means maintaining a most delicate and complex balance in which our leverage in the Sino-Soviet relationship is perforce limited.

What are the implications of such a strategic posture for U.S. export controls? The issue does not revolve around exports of arms and fissionable materials, the sale of which is legally banned to Communist countries by both the United States and our allies. The problem arises in relation to the transfer of advanced technology, materials, and equipment which can have military applications. It is in this context that U.S. export controls are currently based on the principle of equidistance in relation to China and the Soviet Union.

The widely prevailing assumption is that equidistance automatically favors China without embarrassing us in our relationship with the Soviet Union. This is supposedly the case since the Russians are technologically much more advanced than the Chinese. Thus to the extent that the Soviets seek to purchase strategic items abroad, these will tend to be technologically the most advanced. If their shipment to the U.S.S.R. is approved, and we follow a policy of equidistance, it correspondingly makes them actually or potentially available to the PRC.

However, the technological gap between the Soviets and the Chinese might create many situations in which the policy of equidistance could penalize the Chinese, at least unwittingly. Precisely because the Soviets are technologically more advanced, they can produce at home a wide range of items which may be classified as strategic by COCOM and/or the United States. Under such circumstances the Soviets would have no reason to seek the purchase of such products abroad. The crucial question then becomes: Would such strategic items be licensed for shipment to China or would the policy of equidistance be interpreted in such a way that these goods would be denied to the PRC?

Both the logic of the situation and the strategic interests of the United States would suggest that the licensing of such items for export to the PRC can be easily justified. As a matter of fact, one could argue that for the reasons outlined above it would be to our strategic advantage to interpret the policy of equidistance as liberally as possible and license for export to the Chinese all items that are available to the Soviets, regardless of how acquired. This does not necessarily mean that all such items need to be exported from the United States. On the contrary, there may be many situations in which, from a diplomatic, technical or economic point of view, it might be more convenient that such products or technology be sold to the PRC by Japan, the United Kingdom, or some other West European country. This is precisely what happened in 1975 with the $200 million sale of Spey jet engines by Britain to China; the engines can be used in both commercial and military aircraft. With this precedent established, similar deals ought to be encouraged by us in the future. As a matter of fact this may already be happening, as evidenced by some recent shifts in U.S. policy, most clearly illustrated by the tentative approval of an export license for the sale of a highly advanced computer to China. Such a policy shift makes sense in purely practical terms as well since, if the Soviets can and do produce the kinds of strategic items referred to above, they could under some circumstances become in any case available to the Chinese—if not directly from Russia then from Eastern Europe.

This brief review suggests that there are basically three types of institutional obstacles to the further expansion of the Sino-American trade. The first is rooted in our inability to grant intermediate or long-term credits to the Chinese, even assuming that they were prepared to accept them. The second relates to our export control policy, and the third is conditioned by the absence of formal diplomatic relations, which not only affects trade indirectly in the ways outlined above but more directly as well.

Thus it cannot be pure coincidence that Sino-American trade was expanding rapidly while our relations with China were improving and has been contracting since relations have been marking time. There is no question that the sudden rise in our exports to China, followed by a marked curtailment, was in part induced by the economic factors explored in the preceding section. But almost certainly, when the Chinese required additional grain and other farm products, they purchased these from the United States not only because it was easily obtainable here but also as a demonstration of their commitment to better Sino-American relations. Correspondingly, when a succession of good harvests enabled the Chinese to curtail their farm imports, they shifted the whole burden of reduction to the United States. This was in part due to their long-term grain-purchasing agreements with Canada and Australia, combined with some of the quality problems encountered in American grain shipments referred to earlier. Yet it also served as a signal of their displeasure at the slow progress in the normalization of relations between the two countries.

This conclusion is reinforced by China's stance toward all

[91]

forms of exchanges—commercial as well as cultural—spelled out to Dr. Kissinger in November 1975 and reiterated at the time of President Ford's visit a month later; namely, that the exchanges are to be frozen at or possibly even slightly below existing levels. This view seems to be buttressed by current projections of Sino-American trade in 1976, for, according to our Department of Commerce, the total turnover of U.S. trade with China will at best be maintained at 1975 levels, with some possible reduction anticipated on the export side.

In sum, there is no doubt that economic considerations have played a major role in shaping the character of Sino-American economic relations since 1971. At the same time, the character of these relations during the past five years clearly demonstrates that it is strongly influenced by foreign policy factors as well, so much so that full normalization of diplomatic relations may be considered a necessary precondition for wholly normal and sustained trade relations.

The experience of other countries may be instructive in testing this proposition. As shown before, China's foreign trade rose rapidly after about 1970 under the combined impact of domestic development and a more open foreign trade orientation. This was also the period during which a number of countries established formal diplomatic relations with Peking. For 14 of these there are continuous trade figures before and after 1970. If one takes for comparison the level of exports in the year preceding diplomatic recognition and then in 1974, in the cases of Canada, Japan, Germany, Italy and Spain, exports to China did not increase more rapidly (in some cases less rapidly) than total non-Communist world exports to the PRC over these intervals On the other hand, nine countries exhibited appreciably faster trade growth with the PRC following recognition than did the non-Communist world as a whole for equivalent periods. While this evidence is far from conclusive, it does suggest a definite correlation between the establishment of formal diplomatic relations and trade expansion.

U.S.-China Trade Prospects

Given the imponderables of China's future economic and trade policies, particularly in the post-Mao era, and the uncertainties surrounding the course of Sino-American relations, it is not possible to project the level of U.S.-China trade five or ten years hence. Despite a number of attempts to do so, often couched in highly optimistic terms, [14] it seems to me that at best one can outline some hypothetical possibilities and analyze some of the factors that may affect the course of China's trade in years to come.

As noted earlier, China's GNP has apparently been rising at an average annual rate of 6 percent, while imports have been growing at about 5 percent in constant prices between 1952 and 1974. Assuming that China's import needs in the future would grow at the same rate, its total purchases from abroad would rise from approximately $7.5 billion in 1975 to about $9.6 billion in 1980 and $12.2 billion in 1985 (in terms of 1975 dollars). It is extremely difficult even to conjecture what the U.S. share of such Chinese import orders might be. If the United States were to attain the same importance in China's imports as it did at its peak in 1974 (i.e., 13 percent), then our sales to the PRC could amount to about $1.25 billion in 1980 and $1.6 billion in 1985 (in constant dollars). On the other hand, if our position in China's trade recedes to the 1975-76 position (i.e., 4 percent of total PRC imports), then the corresponding figures will be close to $400 million in 1980 and $500 million in 1985.

Given a limited market for Chinese products even if all the institutional obstacles referred to earlier were to be removed, the lower figures may be considered more probable if the Chinese will feel compelled to seek a more or less balanced trade with the United States. On the other hand, if they can find ways of removing the balance-of-payment constraints, then U.S. exports of over $1 billion by 1980 and 1985 do not seem at all improbable.

Between 1975 and 1980 China will have to finance not only its current imports but repay the medium-term credits incurred in 1973 and 1974 by its program of $2.5 billion in complete plant purchases. This will require annual repayments ranging from $220 million to $370 million in various years and thus, to this extent at least, aggravate the country's balance-of-payments burden.[15] There are several ways in which the Chinese could relieve these balance-of-payment pressures. They could seek additional credits, including long-term commercial loans from the world banking community, and/or they could try to step up more rapidly their oil exports.

Contracting of long-term banking loans would require a far-reaching change in China's economic policy. Thus far the policy of self-reliance has been interpreted as being compatible with deferred payments or suppliers' credits on a short-term or medium-term (usually five years) basis. Foreign bank loans were usually disguised as foreign currency deposits in the Bank of China on an annual (or shorter-term) basis, earning interest and often renewable. This form of financing trade deficits or loan repayments may be continued and may serve to solve part of the problem. To this should be added the possibility that if and when diplomatic and economic relations between the United States and the People's Republic are fully normalized and the unresolved issues discussed in the preceding section of this chapter are settled, China could gain access to American Export-Import Bank credits as well as to private bank financing, which could be substantial.

Under some special combination of circumstances one could envisage a substantial expansion in Sino-American trade, beyond the limits indicated above. This could take place if full normalization of relations, removal of all the significant institutional barriers to trade and financing, an active program of investment and economic expansion within China coupled with a renewed demand for U.S. agricultural products, and a rapid rise of oil exports from the PRC could all be achieved at one and the same time. If all these conditions were to prevail, one could visualize the United States supplying 20 percent or more of China's total import orders. In that case, and following the assumption of a continuing trend rate of growth in PRC imports of about 5 percent as spelled out above, U.S. sales to China could rise to as much as $2 billion by 1980 (more than double the peak 1974 level) and about $2.5 billion by 1985.

Unfortunately the probability of all of these conditions being met at the same time must be considered as fairly remote. One could easily sketch an alternative scenario with at least equal plausibility. China at present is caught in the throes of a succession struggle which has become aggravated following the deaths of Chou and Mao. This could have short-term destabilizing effects on the economy, reflected in a slowing-down in the rate of expansion. This in itself would most probably lead to a reduction in the rate of growth of import demand and export supply. Although such a reduction could be reinforced if the succession struggle were to produce a renewed emphasis on self-reliance and a more narrow and strict reinterpretation of this concept, this possibility has been greatly reduced by the remarkably rapid purge of the "leftist" leaders and the apparent success of the more moderate leadership following Mao's death.

[95]

Irrespective of these considerations, how likely is it that China will again enter U.S. farm markets to purchase large quantities of wheat, cotton, soybeans and some other products? As indicated above, China bought 3 million to 4 million tons of grain from us in 1973 and 1974, with total agricultural purchases valued at around $650 million. These purchases ceased when China curtailed its farm imports, placing the whole burden of these reductions on the United States and thereby treating it as a residual supplier. With this history, it is quite possible, or even probable, that should the Chinese experience another really poor harvest they would seek American farm products to replenish their reserves. However, in the absence of any long-term arrangements, the Chinese may be incurring considerable risks; they may wish to enter U.S. markets at a time of very tight world grain supplies and higher prices. Under some circumstances, they could experience considerable difficulty in obtaining these foodstuffs in the quantities required by them. Given these risks, one could imagine that following full normalization of diplomatic relations the Chinese might wish to conclude with us multiyear farm purchase contracts based on the Canadian and Australian models.

Our hypothetical projections of U.S. exports to China can be summarized in the following tabulation, with the various alternatives based on the assumption that total Chinese imports will continue to grow at an average annual rate of 5 percent over the next ten years.

	In billions of 1975 dollars	
	1980	1985
Assuming a PRC import share of:		
4 percent from the U.S.	0.38	0.49
13 percent from the U.S.	1.25	1.59
20 percent from the U.S.	1.92	2.44

The first of these possibilities is based on the 1975-76 trade patterns, while the second reflects the experience of 1973-74. The last is intended to represent an upper limit under the most favorable combination of circumstances.

As indicated above, what the level of future American sales to China may actually turn out to be will largely depend upon the course of PRC economic policies and development patterns, the state of our bilateral political relations, the availability of credits for financing possible trade deficits, China's demand for agricultural imports, and, last but not least, the rate of growth of its oil exports. Except for the oil question, these issues were discussed in the preceding pages of this essay.

Until the 1960s it was generally thought that China was poorly endowed with oil resources. As part of the self-reliance policy and to free themselves from dependence on the Soviet Union, the Chinese then embarked on a most active program of geological exploration. This led to the discovery of sizable deposits of oil in the North and Northeast of China, the Pohai Gulf, and offshore along the continental shelf. As a result, crude oil production has been rising in excess of 20 percent annually, from a mere 5 million tons a year in 1961 to 77 million in 1975.[16] Consequently, China became self-sufficient in oil around the mid-1960s and began to export it in commercial quantities in 1973. These exports rose to about 6.5 million tons in 1974 and an estimated 10 to 11 million tons in 1975.[17]

Japan was the principal market for Chinese oil, with about 1 million tons shipped in 1973, 4.5 million tons in 1974, and 7.8 million in 1975. The rest went to North Korea, Vietnam, Hong Kong, Thailand and the Philippines. These 1975 oil sales were valued at around $850 million, thus comprising 12 to 13 percent of China's total exports. It was generally expected that oil exports would continue to grow rapidly, with

Japan serving as the largest customer. It was estimated that by 1980 China would export between 30 million to 50 million tons of oil, with both Japanese and Chinese sources encouraging such estimates. Even the lower figure would yield export earnings of $2.2 billion to $2.6 billion in terms of 1975 prices. This in itself would serve to relieve balance-of-payment pressures, thus enabling China to pursue an active import program. It should also enable China to finance fairly sizable trade deficits with the United States. Therefore such an outlook could create rather favorable prospects for our exports to the PRC.

A number of more recent indications suggest that these projections were perhaps over-optimistic. A recently published and detailed study of China's energy balance demonstrates that the country's domestic energy needs are likely to grow more rapidly than was previously estimated. At the same time, it is most doubtful that the exceptionally rapid rates of oil production growth experienced in the last ten to fifteen years can be sustained over the next five to ten years.[18] These doubts seem to be borne out by a number of reports from Chinese official sources in the first half of 1976 that suggest a slowing-down in the rate of extraction. On the basis of the available information at present it is impossible to tell whether these slow-downs reflect changes in economic policy with a reduced emphasis on investments in oil production and exports, temporary technical problems, or changes in methods of extraction.

In recent months, complications also seem to be developing on the oil export front. Rather unexpectedly the Chinese reduced their oil shipments to Japan in 1976, and the negotiations for a long-term oil export agreement are tentatively providing for guaranteed Japanese purchases of only 15 million to 18 million tons rather than the 30 million to 50 million talked about earlier.[19] In part, these changes in signals may reflect a Sino-Japanese bargaining process concerning price and other terms of the agreement, but they may reflect more fundamental problems as well.

In any case, based on the aforementioned CIA study, it would seem quite doubtful that China could spare oil export surpluses of more than 30 million tons by 1980. These amounts could be raised significantly if China were prepared to enter into co-production or similar types of arrangements with the international oil companies to accelerate offshore drilling in deep waters. The Chinese have repeatedly emphasized their strong opposition to such agreements, and it is most improbable that this policy is likely to be changed in the foreseeable future.

What are the implications of these oil production and export trends for Sino-American trade prospects? Supposing that PRC oil exports would indeed be around 30 million tons in 1980, is any of this oil likely to be sold to the United States? Based on the experience of recent years, China's oil markets seem to be in Asia, particularly in Japan. However if the Japanese were to buy only half of China's oil export surpluses in 1980, it is conceivable that the Chinese might seek to enter the U.S. market. Were this to occur, it would provide a basis for a sizable growth of both American imports from and exports to China, as pointed out earlier. But all the current indications are that our oil companies have shown no interest in importing Chinese oil into the United States because of its high cost and its particular quality characteristics. Their interest seems to have been focused on co-production or various types of marketing arrangements through which they could gain some kind of control over Chinese oil exports; through these, they could send them to different destinations based on their own world marketing strategy. Not too surprisingly, the Chinese have shown little interest in either of these possibilities.

For all of these reasons the probabilities of Chinese oil exports to the United States cannot be rated as high in the foreseeable future. But the lack of a bilateral balance in Sino-American trade need not by itself preclude a significant expansion in U.S. exports to the PRC, as was shown earlier, provided that the Chinese find some means for balancing their total trade and/or relieving the pressures on their balance of payments. In this respect, exports of even 30 million tons of oil can play an important role. This would roughly treble China's 1975 oil exports and thus could add about $1.7 billion to the PRC's foreign exchange earnings in 1980 (at 1975 prices).

Under these assumptions, the PRC could cover its current trade deficits, meet its debt repayments resulting from its complete plant purchases, and have about $1 billion left for additional purchases abroad. If all of these additional resources were to be channeled into purchases from the United States, while our current exports to the PRC continued to grow at the same average rate as assumed for total Chinese imports (5 percent), our sales could rise to about $1.4 billion by 1980. This would roughly correspond to the intermediate possibility sketched in the tabulation above. However, the probability that all of this additional $1 billion would be diverted to the American market must be considered extremely low. Therefore, realistically and even under reasonably favorable assumptions of diplomatic and trade normalization, U.S. exports to China are more likely to be somewhere within a $500 million to $1 billion range by 1980. These figures are projected in terms of 1975 dollars and can of course be expected to be higher in 1980 in terms of then prevailing export prices. They may also be raised should the PRC decide to enter U.S. farm markets and become a more or less regular market for our agricultural products, particularly following full normalization of our diplomatic relations.

Thus the volume of Sino-American trade five to ten years hence could vary considerably in view of the many elements—political and diplomatic as well as economic—that will influence the course of relations between the two countries. Yet even if the more dramatic possibilities spelled out above are not realized, Sino-American trade will be one of the key elements in the bilateral relationship between the two countries, and will present both governments with policy choices that will have an important impact on the totality of their relationship.

NOTES

1. These ratios are necessarily subject to sizable margins of error arising from several sources. The GNP estimates for China are subject to considerable uncertainty. Moreover, these are derived in Chinese prices expressed in yuan values. However, China's foreign trade has to be reconstructed from the trading partner side, all expressed in U.S. dollars. It is far from clear at what rates these dollars should be converted into yuan, that is, whether it should be the official exchange rate or some estimated purchasing power parity rates. Depending on what conversion method is used, China's foreign trade ratios could range between 2 and 20 percent. More realistically, they probably fall within a 4 to 8 percent range.

The data are from the United Nations, *Statistical Yearbook, 1974* (New York, 1975), pp. 406-13 and 644-46. Data from China are from A. Eckstein, *Communist China's Economic Growth and Foreign Trade* (New York, 1966), Table 4-9, pp. 120-21, and from A.G. Ashbrook, Jr., "China, Economic Overview, 1975," in *China, A Reassessment of the Economy*, A Compendium of Papers Submitted to the Joint Economic Committee, 94th Congress, lst Session, July 10, 1975, Table 2, p. 23; those for the Soviet Union are from F.D. Holzman, "Foreign Trade", in Abram Bergson and Simon Kuznets (eds.): *Economic Trends in the Soviet Union* (Cambridge, Mass., 1963), Table VII.3, p. 290.

2. Based on an as yet unpublished study by Robert Michael Field, *Real Capital Formation in the People's Republic of China: 1952-1973* (April 1976), Table 8, p. 30 and Table 19, p. 60.

3. A. Eckstein, *Communist China's Economic Growth and Foreign Trade* (New York, 1966), p. 124.

4. *Ibid.,* pp. 127-28.

5. "Report on the Work of the Government," *Peking Review,* No. 4 (January 24, 1975), pp. 23-25.

6. CIA Research Aid, *People's Republic of China: International Trade Handbook* (Washington, D.C., October 1976), pp. 21-23.

7. Foreign Broadcast Information Service (FBIS), *PRC Daily Broadcast,* Vol. I, No. 203 (October 18, 1974).

8. A.L. Erisman, "China, Agriculture in the 1970s," in *China, A Reassessment, op. cit.,* Tables 3 and 4, pp. 343-44.

9. Steven C. Haas, *Impact of MFN on U.S. Imports from the PRC,* Office of East-West Trade, Department of State (August 1973), mimeo.

10. David Denny, *The Effect of Normalized Commercial Relations on PRC Exports to the U.S.,* Bureau of East-West Trade, Department of Commerce (1973), mimeo.

11. See Charles H. Bayar, "China's Frozen Assets in the U.S., Their Present Status and Future Disposition," in *U.S.-China Business Review,* No. 5, Vol. 2 (September-October 1975).

12. *The Asian Wall Street Journal,* September 7, 1976, p. 2.

13. These issues were perhaps most clearly laid out in an article by Michael Pillsbury, "U.S.-Chinese Military Ties," *Foreign Policy,* No. 20 (Fall 1975).

14. See the statement of the Hon. Christopher H. Phillips in *United States-China Relations: The Process of Normalization of Relations,* Hearings before the Special Subcommittee on Investigations of the Committee on International Relations, House of Representatives, 94th Congress (Washington, 1976), pp. 76 and 86.

15. Based on David L. Denny, "China's Foreign Financial Liabilities," in *U.S.-China Business Review,* Vol. 2, No. 1 (January-February 1975), Table 2, p. 37.

16. See Bobby Williams, "The Chinese Petroleum Industry, Growth and Prospects," in *China, A Reassessment, op. cit.,* p. 28; and National Council for U.S.-China Trade, *China's Petroleum Industry* (Washington, D.C., 1976), p. 25.

17. Bobby Williams, *ibid.,* pp. 239-41.

18. CIA, Research Aid, *China, Energy Balance Projections* (Washington, D.C., November 1975).

19. The figure of 15-18 million tons is based on a *Japan Economic Journal* news item, Vol. 14, No. 683 (January 27, 1976), p. 5; the 30-50 million tons is based on my article, "China's Trade Policy and Sino-American Relations," *Foreign Affairs,* Vol. 54, No. 1 (October 1975).

APPENDIX

Highlights of U.S.-China Trade

July 1969

Trade and travel restrictions relaxed, allowing travel to China by certain categories of U.S. citizens, and permitting the purchase for noncommercial use of up to $100 worth of goods originating in the PRC.

December 1969

Regulations relaxed, permitting U.S. subsidiaries and affiliates abroad to sell nonstrategic goods to China and buy Chinese products for resale on foreign markets, and removing the $100 ceiling on Chinese goods bought by Americans for noncommercial use.

March 1970

Passport regulations changed to allow travel to China by Americans "for any legitimate purpose."

April 1970 — President authorized shipment of American-made components in nonstrategic, foreign-manufactured goods.

August 1970 — State Department dropped requirement that free-world ships engaged in trade with China may not use bunkering or fueling facilities owned by American firms unless a check shows the ships are not carrying strategic goods.

March 1971 — Travel requirements lifted, allowing travel by Americans to PRC.

June 1971 — President announced a list of commodities that could be freely traded with China, and Treasury's foreign assets control regulations on PRC removed, allowing PRC imports (with the exception of the seven embargoed furs) entry into the U.S.

January 1, 1972 — U.S.-China Trade for 1971: U.S. imports from the PRC totaled $4.9 million. Since all trade was indirect, there are no figures for U.S. exports to the PRC.

February 24, 1972 — PRC was placed on the same level as the Soviet Union for export control purposes, which meant that goods exportable to the Soviet Union without explicit approval of the Department of Commerce could also be exported to China under general license.

February 28, 1972 — Shanghai Communiqué, issued at the culmination of the President's visit, announced that both the United States and China would begin working toward fa-

	cilitating the progressive development of trade.
April 1972	PRC for the first time invited 36 American firms to attend the Spring Chinese Export Commodities Fair held in Canton. American purchases at the fair represented the first direct trade between the two countries since 1949.
November 1972	U.S. Department of Commerce and Transportation jointly announced the relaxation of restrictions on U.S. carriers to call on Chinese ports.
January 1, 1973	U.S.-China trade for 1972: U.S. imports from China totaled $32.4 million; U.S. exports to China totaled $63.5 million.
February 22, 1973	Communiqué announced the establishment of Liaison Offices by the United States and China in their respective capitals.
March 15, 1973	President announced the appointment of David K.E. Bruce as head of U.S. Liaison Office in Peking.
March 22, 1973	First meeting of Executive Committee of the National Council for U.S.-China Trade.
March 30, 1973	PRC announced appointment of Huang Chen as head of Liaison Office in Washington.
April 5, 1973	Five-man advance party headed by Alfred le S. Jenkins, Deputy Chief of the U.S. Liaison Office, arrived in China to

prepare for the opening of this office.

April 18, 1973   Ten-man advance party headed by Han Hsu, Deputy Chief of the PRC Liaison Office, arrived in Washington to prepare for the opening of this office.

May 14, 1973   U.S. Liaison Office in Peking opened.

May 31, 1973   Inauguration of the National Council for U.S.-China Trade.

Sept.-Oct. 1973   For the first time, U.S. businessmen at the Kwangchow Fair are serviced by two office suites staffed with U.S. government personnel and by the National Council.

November 1973   Board members of National Council constitute first commercial American delegation to visit China.

January 1, 1974   U.S.-China Trade for 1973: U.S. imports from the PRC, $64.9 million; exports to the PRC, $740.2 million; total trade, $811.7 million.

June 6, 1974   Secretary Kissinger and Ambassador Huang attend first anniversary celebration of the National Council; Kissinger reaffirms U.S. policy toward the PRC. Council membership stands at 215.

September 4, 1974   President announced appointment of George Bush as head of U.S. Liaison Office in Peking.

Oct.-Nov. 1974   American firms in attendence at the Kwangchow Fair reached 220; estimated business done surpassed $40 million.

January 1, 1975   U.S.-China trade for 1974: U.S. imports

| | from the PRC, $114.7 million; exports to the PRC, $819.1 million; total trade, $933.8 million. |
| Feb.-March 1975 | PRC textile delegation to the U.S. represents the first China trade mission to the U.S. |

Source: U.S. Department of Commerce, Domestic and International Business Administration, Bureau of East-West Trade.

[FOUR]

Building a Relationship on the Sands of Cultural Exchanges

Lucian W. Pye

Right from the outset the Shanghai Communiqué proclaimed that the new Sino-American relationship was to be built upon officially blessed cultural exchanges: "The two sides agreed that it is desirable to broaden the understanding between the two peoples. To this end, they discussed specific areas in such fields as science, technology, culture, sports and journalism, in which people-to-people contacts and exchanges would be mutually beneficial. Each side undertakes to facilitate the further development of such contacts and exchanges."

And of all the activities that have followed upon the new openings in relations, cultural exchanges have been the easiest for both Peking and Washington to justify and publicly extol. While some observers suspect that since 1972 more substantial accomplishments have been made in the realm of trade, it has not been politic for either government to publicize the unlikely fact that businessmen have turned out to be the most natural bridge between ideologically antagonistic social systems. It is somewhat awkward to explain why capitalists should be so eager to strengthen a Communist system, or why devout believers in self-sufficiency and human willpower are so ready to deal with foreign merchants of technology. So it has been more convenient for each government to praise cultural exchanges, and actively support them.

This ease of common agreement is, in the light of history, paradoxical, for in the past some of the most troublesome problems in Sino-American relations lay precisely in the realm of culture. For over 150 years the Chinese have felt threatened by Western culture, and in more recent years the United States has spent fortunes to keep the "culture" of the Chinese Communists from spreading. Now both Washington and Peking seem to welcome each other's culture, and each has committed itself to facilitate the growth of cultural exchanges.

The subject of cultural exchange has provided much of the small talk accompanying the "substantive discussions" that have been the presumed objectives of presidential visits and Secretary Henry Kissinger's trips to China. And, indeed, when the Secretary or the President are pushed by the press to specify the concrete accomplishments of their travels, they invariably mention progress in cultural exchanges.

Spoilsports, however, belittle exchanges as both pretentious and absurd: pretentious because they have been so limited and asymmetrical; absurd because, in their view, neither the People's Republic of China nor the United States have "cultures" worthy of "exchanging." The history of Communist rule has been a largely unrelieved effort to erase the cultural accomplishments of one of the world's greatest civilizations and to replace it with adolescent enthusiasm and the grotesqueries of propaganda art. And as for the cultural limitations of America, they are too numerous and well known to need any elaboration—or so say the spoilsports.

Truth does require the modest concession that "cultural exchange" is an umbrella euphemism covering a variety of activities, many of which lie at the margin, if not beyond the limits, of conventional definitions of "culture." Indeed, the diversity is such that it is treacherous to treat "cultural exchange" as a coherent activity. This diversity also means that policy makers and participants in the exchanges in both countries have quite different interests in different parts of the program. Therefore, before we explore the problems of policy in cultural exchanges it will be helpful to note something of the variety of activities which have already become the mainstays of exchanges.

In identifying the aspects of current cultural exchange programs it is appropriate to begin with sports, for, after all, the public signal for opening the new phase in relations between the two countries was Peking's invitation to the American ping-pong team to visit China for some "friendly games." The National Committee on U.S.-China Relations—one of the two principal American agents for "facilitated" exchanges (a category explained below)—got its start in this field by quickly offering to help sponsor a return invitation to the Chinese ping-pong team to tour the United States. Since then, American swimmers, track and field athletes, and basketball players have gone to China, and Chinese gymnasts and a woman's basketball team have been received in this country.[1] Although it would be naïve to idealize the "bridge-building" potential of sports, the appearances of American teams before large audiences have served to inform more Chinese than any other type of "cultural exchange" that it is now politically permissible to cheer Americans and to observe that they are not as decadent as Chinese official propaganda only recently painted them. Furthermore, because the Chinese have gone to great lengths to emphasize "friendship" and play down competition, goodwill has been encouraged among participants. (The Chinese anxiety to ensure that everyone can be a winner and no one's feelings need be hurt has given American athletes an experience which most have not had since they went to mother-managed birthday parties where everybody "won" something.)

Closely related to athletic exchanges are those in the performing arts and various forms of "spectaculars." They have included visits of acrobats and Chinese "martial arts" and operatic troupes, and a trip to China by the Philadelphia Symphony Orchestra. This last and a Chinese archaeological exhibit were exchanges that should satisfy even the purist about "culture." Unfortunately, they may have been the high points in this category of exchange. In China the remaining forms of public entertainment are revolutionary operas and ballets that are heavy with propaganda and the musical performances that occur at what the Chinese are wont to call "soirées." Performed by a soloist or a small group, these instrumental or vocal numbers are reminiscent of the era predating Nelson Eddy and Jeanette MacDonald, in the sense that male and female perform separately and don't sing with or to each other.

Sports and "spectaculars" are the two general categories which require audiences and hence some degree of publicity. All the other forms of cultural exchanges are built around the concept of visiting "delegations," which blend tourism with "briefings" and "discussions" with opposite numbers and appropriate officials.

American delegations going to China have largely been of

two types: (1) groups of notables such as college presidents, world affairs specialists, congressmen; and (2) groups of scientific and academic specialists such as doctors (especially those in aspects of public health), computer scientists, geologists and earthquake experts, and various types of technologists.

These are the primary categories of activities covered in the cultural exchanges; because the two governments have in some measure negotiated them, they are therefore referred to as "facilitated" exchanges. The National Committee on U.S.-China Relations has had responsibilities for sports, the performing arts, and citizen delegations; the Committee on Scholarly Exchanges with the People's Republic of China (representing the National Academy of Sciences, the Social Science Research Council, and the American Council of Learned Societies) has responsibilities for the scientific and academic exchanges. The latter have mainly involved the physical sciences and technical fields and only marginally the social sciences and humanities.

Outside the area of these mutually recognized activities, the Chinese have unilaterally invited many American delegations and individuals to visit China. In addition, the Chinese have encouraged the founding of Chinese-American Friendship Associations in numerous American cities, and have greatly augmented the attractiveness of these associations by favoring their members with visas for visits to China. Although these initiatives of the Chinese have made it possible for many Americans to learn more about some aspects of China, they do not properly fall in the domain of cultural exchanges as envisaged in the Shanghai Communiqué. These unilateral programs of the Chinese have a strong political public relations cast; which is not at all to say that the Americans who have traveled to China under them are necessarily politically sympathetic to the Peking regime—indeed, the vast majority are probably only curious or are emotionally attracted to the lot of the Chinese people.

Needless to say, the United States government has not sought to penetrate Chinese society in the same way; and if it tried it would certainly fail, and would also probably compromise whoever might be singled out for an invitation. Both the Chinese and American authorities recognize that there are "basic differences in our two social systems": America is an open society, so therefore what the Chinese are doing unilaterally in contacting American citizens is legitimate; whereas China is a closed society and hence it would be improper for outsiders to contact individual Chinese directly.

Thus we can think of the flow of people in terms of three main channels. First, there is the "facilitated" exchange channel, which is the only two-way channel since it involves Americans going to China and Chinese coming to the United States. Second, there is the *ad hoc* channel wherein individuals or groups of Americans are invited directly by the Chinese; and the third is the Friendship Association channel. Both of these last are, of course, one-way channels from the United States to China.

For the reasons given above, it is correct to think of cultural *exchanges* as involving only those activities associated with the "facilitated" exchanges. Progress in cultural exchanges therefore has to be measured solely in terms of developments under the "facilitated" exchange programs. Of course, some of the goals of cultural exchange "to broaden the understanding between the two peoples" can be furthered by "friendship" activities, and therefore they need not be inconsistent with the program of "facilitated" exchanges. But if the facilitated exchange programs should fail to grow and if political strains should creep into the relations between the two governments, hen the Chinese "friendship" activities might be seen in a ifferent, and less constructive, light.

In the meantime, any analysis of the policy problem in dvancing cultural exchanges must begin with the recognition hat the Chinese are operating at two levels while the United tates government is adhering only to the one level of facilitated" exchanges. This existential fact does have conse-quences for the negotiation of exchange programs since the Chinese, often having alternative possibilities, are at times under less compelling pressures. Washington officials, ac-nowledging that this situation exists, nevertheless feel that the Chinese do have an interest in the success of "facilitated" xchanges. The Chinese understand that these are the only xchanges relevant to the growth of intergovernmental rela-ions, and there are certain things which the Chinese would ke to do, especially in sending performing groups to this ountry, that can only be accomplished with the cooperation f the U.S. government. How valid these judgments will prove o be can only be answered with the passage of time. For the resent, at least, the Chinese seem pleased to have the dvantages of the two levels.

While it is incontrovertible that the facilitated exchanges re the only relevant measure for determing the relative upport of each side for the "spirit of the Shanghai Communi-ué" on cultural exchanges, it must be recognized that this hannel has the smallest number of people. From 1971 to the nd of 1975, between 7,000 and 9,000 Americans visited China—and about one-half of these were Chinese-Americans—ut of this total only 554 traveled under facilitated exchange rrangements.

For Chinese coming to America the facilitated exchanges ave been relatively more important, accounting for 454 isitors out of a total of 651 through 1975.

If we eliminate the large numbers in "tourism" and "friendship" visits to China and focus only on the numbers of scholars, we find much the same pattern. Ninety percent of the Chinese scholars who have come to the United States traveled under the sponsorship of the Committee on Scholarly Communications with the People's Republic of China (CSCPRC), while only about a quarter of the American scholars who have been to China went under facilitated arrangements.[2]

Before looking more closely at specific problems in advancing cultural exchanges, we need to take note of another existential fact which profoundly colors the dynamics of exchanges. I am referring to certain broad cultural, rather than political, differences, which affect the process of exchange but which lie beyond the influences of policy makers.

THE "MIDDLE KINGDOM COMPLEX" AND "MARCO POLO-ITIS"

The development of cultural exchanges between China and America has been informed in the broadest sense by quite different sets of mind in the two countries, which, miracle of miracles, complement each other. If there is a paradox in the current enthusiasm of both governments for cultural exchanges when contrasted with the immediately preceding period, there has been remarkable consistency in attitudes when seen against a longer historical tradition.

Many observers have been struck by the extent to which the present-day rulers in Peking seem to share the historic beliefs of Chinese that they are the center of the world, that it is entirely natural that foreigners would travel expectantly from afar to be properly awed by the wonders of China, and that presidents and prime ministers, secretaries of state and foreign ministers, should await the convenience of China's supreme ruler for audiences, just as tribute missions in the past came before the Chinese emperor. And these attitudes fail to grate on American nerves because Americans are infected with the uncontrollable excitement which accompanies any prospect of traveling to Cathay, a fever to which Westerners have been susceptible since they first heard of the expoits of Marco Polo.

When American delegations listen attentively to the words of leading cadres and vice-premiers to learn about the latest wonders of Chinese ingenuity, it is possible to hear echoes of the phrases and sentiments earlier Chinese mandarins and emperors used to instruct British and other Western missions seeking to normalize relations with Peking. For example, delegations being told by the responsible cadres of a revolutionary committee that they only want to improve their management and "serve the people" seem to be listening to a present-day rendition of Emperor Ch'ien Lung's declaration to Lord Macartney: "I have but one aim in view, namely to maintain a perfect governance and to fulfill the duties of the state." When American visitors are surprised that their Chinese hosts are so indifferent to the latest things in the world at large, they seem to be facing again the Chinese emperor's scorn: "Strange and costly objects from afar do not interest me." And when President Ford is advised by Vice-Premier Teng Hsiao-p'ing that he should shore up NATO, not allow the Soviets to gain military superiority, and unite the American people for the coming struggle, we seem to be hearing again the Chia Ch'ing emperor's instruction to Lord Jeffrey Amherst for King George III: "For the future, O King, if you will keep your subjects in order and strengthen your national defenses, I shall hold you in high esteem, notwithstanding your remoteness."

In contrast to the inward-looking mood of the Chinese there is in America today greater interest in China than in any other foreign country. It is currently a status symbol among American opinion makers to have traveled to China, and by all indications there will be no slackening in the quest for visas for some time. One delegation after another comes back to report that they too have seen the same sights—toured the Great Wall, the Ming Tombs, the Forbidden City, and possibly the Gardens of Hangchow; visited the same communes, factories, neighborhood committees, nursery schools and industrial exhibitions; attended identical briefings about economic planning, educational policy, and the contrast between before and after "liberation" in the people's livelihood. Apparently, the more Americans hear the same accounts, the more the craving to visit China grows.

Such attitudes give Peking advantages in the negotiation of cultural exchanges. For the individual American, impatient to visit China, it makes little difference whether he is a part of a "facilitated" exchange or a "friendship" arrangement. Chinese negotiators can be confident that a large dose of tourism and sight-seeing will leave most American delegations gratified, even if there has been little in the way of substantive or professional discussions. Above all, the Chinese are in a position to make it appear that it is they who are making gracious concessions by allowing others to visit them. The implicit logic of the situation is thus that the foreigners are in need of that which China alone can offer.

These attitudes characterize in general the structure of the exchange situation. On closer examination, however, we find countervailing considerations which negate some of Peking's advantages. The usual procedure in negotiating the cultural exchange "package" for each year is that Americans propose a large number of possibilities and the Chinese decide which ones will, in fact, make up the year's program—a procedure consistent with the general structure of attitudes. Yet, at the point of decision, it turns out that it is the Chinese who have strong preferences and urgent priorities, while the United States government is essentially indifferent. To be specific, the Chinese look to exchanges to provide technological knowledge and the legitimizing effects of broad publicity.

In short, the Chinese do in fact hope to use the spirit of the exchanges to yield certain concrete returns, and they are not satisfied with mere abstract sentiments. The United States government, by contrast, is mainly interested in the diffuse sentiments associated with cultural exchanges and has no specific goals which could only be furthered by particular exchange activities. Thus there is a strange array of cross-purposes in the negotiating situation: the Chinese have a general posture of contentment and self-satisfaction, but on specifics they have a strong sense of priorities; while the Americans have a generalized need for advancement in cultural exchanges, but no particular priorities. These circumstances reinforce the tendency for the negotiating process to take the form of the Americans annually offering a smorgasbord of proposed exchanges and the Chinese deciding which ones will take place according to their apparently strong preferences.

This interesting contraposition in the way in which the "Middle Kingdom complex" and "Marco Polo-itis" interact in the sphere of cultural exchanges is also, incidentally, present in the larger context of Chinese diplomatic relations. It might be presumed, for example, that the Chinese should be able to gain great diplomatic advantages out of a situation in which others appear to be seeking the favor of meetings and audiences with Chinese officialdom. Yet if we look to history for analogies, Chinese diplomacy was never more disastrous than when their

[119]

officials were supremely self-satisfied and when foreigners were most anxious to visit their capital. The high point of the Middle Kingdom complex in the past was in the mid-nineteenth century, on the eve of China's near-disintegration. Peking's rulers of that day were hopelessly inept in exploiting any potential advantage. The genius of Chinese diplomacy did not coincide with the classical era of self-satisfaction, when the Chinese felt obligated to be tolerant of the curiosities of less enlightened peoples from across the sea who seemed attracted to the wonders of a "near-perfect" governance. On the contrary, it only emerged when the Chinese, out of their own weaknesses, struck upon the profound insight that foreigners are easiest to handle when they feel compelled by their own sense of pride to presume that they have an obligation to help the Chinese with their "problems."

To digress a bit further, the Chinese talent for using the foreigner's sense of superiority, in combination with their own apparent ineptitude, first emerged in 1858 when the British insisted to the point of war that the Chinese should conform with international usage and at least establish a foreign office. Subsequently, the foreign diplomatic corps took it upon themselves to try to instruct the members of the Tsungli Yamen on the niceties of diplomacy—a nearly hopeless task since the Chinese had staffed their reluctantly established "foreign office" with the least competent officials in the Empire, who always seemed to lose papers and forget the train of discussion from meeting to meeting. To this day, foreigners are frequently puzzled (and at times frustrated) when negotiating with the Chinese because they can never decide whether the strange combination of extreme courtesy and stubbornness they are confronting stems from an inability to grasp what is wanted or is only a calculated tactic.

Historically, Chinese diplomatic successes steadily increased as they played down their "Middle Kingdon" inclinations and fostered the foreigners' sense of superiority, until finally a weak and war-torn China was made one of the Big Five with the veto that went with being a permanent member of the Security Council of the United Nations. Since the establishment of the People's Republic, this same contradiction has been at work: When the Chinese yielded to their sense of greatness and allowed their hubris to carry them to the point of creating that most extrodinary combination of mortal enemies, the United States, the Soviet Union, and India, the country became isolated and its foreign affairs fell into disarray. But then, when they suddenly discovered that they were vulnerable to the Soviet Union and welcomed an opening to the United States, their foreign policy was again touched with genius.

All of this is relevant to cultural exchanges because of what it says about the Chinese negotiating manner and because it reminds us that the Chinese may not necessarily see as "advantages" what others see. They may in fact be troubled by ambivalences. They want to suggest that they have found all the answers to China's problems, but they also want the advantages of advanced international technologies; they want to be self-reliant, but they also want others to help them appear even stronger than they are.

The American approach to cultural exchange is possibly less ambiguous, but we too have our psychological complexes. As noted, American policy makers, in contrast to the Chinese, have no particular preferences or concrete objectives whereby to rank the priorities among the different aspects of cultural exchange. The principal goal of American policy is to suggest that all is going well and according to plan in Sino-American relations; and as long as this is seen as the case, Washington can maintain some leverage on Moscow. Washington is not in

[121]

search of either knowledge or technology from the Chinese. Yet, as part of their objective of keeping the waters smooth, Washington officials do find it necessary to pacify the private American citizens who are the principal clients of cultural exchange, and therefore officials tend to be sympathetic to the scholars, artists, doctors, and other specialists who have legitimate interests in contacts with the Chinese. Their responsiveness, however, can only go to the point of not interfering with their more important concern, which is keeping the Chinese officials in a positive frame of mind toward Washington.

For American citizens, cultural exchanges offer the exciting possibility of learning more about a long-forbidden land; and for some of them, there also seems to be an added dimension of feeling that it is necessary somehow to make amends for the years of enmity between the two countries. For a few Americans, enthusiasm for almost any aspect of exchange becomes a form of *mea culpa* for what they thought went wrong during the McCarthy period. Consequently, there is a widespread American taboo against making any kind of criticism not only of what is learned about China, but also about the manner in which the Chinese conduct their side of exchanges.

Furthermore, the Chinese style in managing exchanges encourages precisely these attitudes among Americans. In addition to their concrete objectives, the Chinese are also inclined to assume that people generally do not make sharp distinctions between cognitive interests and affective orientations. That is, they assume that anyone who is "interested" in China must also have potentially positive feelings about the regime; anyone who might express an apparently critical opinion about anything in China is instantly suspected of being a foe of the regime. As Professor Donald Munro has pointed out, the Chinese tend to "cluster attitudes and feelings."[3] In cultural exchanges this has meant that they have consistently equated "curiosity about Chinese policies" with "friendship toward China," which should then lead directly to having "political sympathies for the People's Republic of China." Most Americans are prepared to go the first two steps, linking their sense of curiosity with an inclination to be "friendly toward," but a good many also feel that such attitudes need not, indeed should not, be confused with any political or ideological identification with the Chinese regime.

This leads to a point which needs to be aired, namely, the suspicion many Americans have about "conducted tours of China" because of gnawing memories of how the early travelers to the Soviet Union made complete fools of themselves by failing to distinguish "show places" from the realities of Stalin's tyranny. The fact that in the 1920s and 1930s there was more freedom for foreigners to travel about in the Soviet Union than in China today adds to the suspicion.

Chinese officials, products of a society permeated by politics, are of course quite aware of the political aspects of cultural exchanges and are hypersensitive to the perceptions of "friends" and "foes." Nevertheless, the Chinese have reasons for wanting to mute the political connotation of exchanges. They recognize that to cater merely to the political enthusiasts of their system would be self-defeating in terms of the larger political objectives they seek in their new opening of relations with the United States.

It should be clear by now that the attitudes and considerations which both Chinese and Americans bring to the building of cultural exchanges are exceedingly complex and at times contradictory. It is necessary to keep these facts in mind as we now consider specific problems which must be effectively dealt with if there is to be further progress in cultural exchanges.

[123]

POLITICAL PRESSURES AND THE ISSUE OF CULTURE

Both the Chinese and American governments approach cultural exchanges in a context of historic as well as contemporary sensitivities to issues about "culture." As noted at the outset, the Chinese have worried for some 150 years about the impact of Western culture on their values—first, on their traditional Confucian values and now on their revolutionary Marxist-Leninist-Maoist values. At the beginning of the twentieth century many Chinese thought they could solve their problems of cultural integrity by relying upon a formula which distinguished between fundamental values and technical, utilitarian knowledge. In a way that epitomized looking down one's nose at Western materialism and praising native spiritual values, they drew the distinction between *t'i*, "essence" or "fundamental values" and *yung*, "utility," "function," or "means." It was appropriate, they argued, to seek to learn Western technology, which was merely *yung*, in order to preserve the *t'i* of Confucian civilization. In the debate which ensued, critics of this view held that the adoption of Western technology would inevitably corrupt traditional values and therefore the dichotomy was false and dangerous.

Today the debate is again taking place in China. Some leaders argue that it is essential to adopt Western technologies to preserve and strengthen China's revolutionary society, while others are fearful that extensive exposure to the outside world will dilute and corrupt its revolutionary values. The terminology is different; instead of *t'i* and *yung*, the current dichotomy is drawn between "red and expert," ideological purity and technical proficiency. Much of China's domestic politics revolves around factions which differ in their emphasis upon "redness" versus "expertness."

[124]

While all Chinese leaders profess support of the Shanghai Communiqué, it is clear that the more ideologically sensitive elements, usually thought of as the "radicals," are not so sure that cultural exchanges, yielding expert knowledge at the possible cost of ideological purity, are in China's national and revolutionary interest. In contrast, those elements most closely identified with the policies of the late Chou En-lai are more interested in finding beneficial possibilities in exchanges and are less anxious about ideological contamination.

All of this is only to say that cultural exchanges are a sensitive issue in Chinese domestic politics and, consequently, could affect basic policy toward the United States. The fall of Madam Mao and the "gang of four" may bring about a less austere approach to cultural affairs in China, which could auger well for a more liberalized program of cultural exchanges. The attack upon the "Shanghai clique" has also brought down the one-time World Table Tennis Champion who was Minister of Sports, and this could help to broaden athletic exchanges. On the other hand, it is too early to be certain about these possibilities because the "moderates," despite their domestic political successes, will still have to be exceedingly careful not to overstep the bounds of revolutionary prudence and appear unduly cavalier about cultural freedom. The fact that China is moving toward greater liberalization in cultural areas is to be welcomed, but the precise boundary of what is and is not acceptable in cultural pursuits remains uncertain and thus fraught with dangers for those who must take responsibilities in designing exchange programs with the capitalistic United States.

For the United States, there also are both political and organizational complications which affect cultural exchanges. The political issue is simply put: while Americans are very sympathetic toward better relations with the People's Republic of China, they also feel troubled about old ties with the government and people on Taiwan. Since this is the subject of another chapter in this book, we need only note here that the election year of 1976 slowed progress toward "normalization" with Peking and hence the Chinese felt justified in freezing the level of cultural exchanges. Since Washington knew that it could not move toward "normalization" until at least after the elections, it also felt that it could not press the Chinese on expanding cultural exchanges.

The organizational issue arises from the fact that a uniquely American combination of public and private institutions have become principals in the "facilitated" exchanges. Both the National Committee on U.S.-China Relations and the Committee on Scholarly Communication with the People's Republic of China are private institutions; the former is a membership organization with an elected board of directors, and the second is sponsored by the three principal learned societies representing the sciences, humanities and social sciences. Each organization makes policies independently of the government, but both are committed to the national objectives of expanding exchanges and both receive government funds for cultural exchanges. Both organizations were established in 1966, long before the Nixon-Kissinger move to open relations with Peking: the National Committee to stimulate public education and policy discussions on U.S.-China relations, and the Committee on Scholarly Communication to explore the possibilities of private contact with Chinese academics. The line between "public" and "private" is thus somewhat ambiguous. Although both organizations cooperate with the Department of State, both have also taken independent positions on certain issues.

The organizational picture is further complicated because each American organization has developed working relations with counterpart groups in China—the CSCPRC with the Chinese Scientific and Technical Association; the National Committee with the Chinese People's Institute, with the Association of Friendship with Foreign Countries, and with the All-China Sports Federation. There are, of course, no doubts about these Chinese organizations being entirely the creatures of the Chinese government. Yet, on certain matters, there may be some degree of difference in interests and emphasis among them. Hence the two American organizations sometimes negotiate directly (or through the American Liaison Office in Peking) with their appropriate counterpart group and at other times they deal with the PRC Liaison Office in Washington.[4]

With these general political and organizational considerations in mind, we may now proceed to examine the more specific issues which have influenced the pattern of cultural exchanges between these organizations and the two countries.

The Selection of Delegations and the Sovereignty of Visa-Granting

An issue fundamental to the healthy growth of cultural exchanges is the question of who decides on the composition of delegations once agreement has been reached that exchanges should take place in a particular field. Viewed in purely legal terms, there is no question whatsoever of the absolute right of sovereign countries to decide who should be allowed into their jurisdictions. Therefore, if the matter were solely a legal or political one, there would be no basis for challenging the right of the receiving country to exclude whomever it wishes for whatever reasons, or lack of reason, it chooses to give. Yet, if cultural exchange is to flourish, the problem of the selection of delegations must also be seen in terms of the principles of propriety and the conventions of courtesy. Furthermore, if exchanges are to be in any way representative of the two cultures, then it would seem essential that the sending side should be allowed to make the decision as to the appropriate membership of its delegation.

Since the advent of "ping-pong" the Chinese have used their legal right to grant and deny visas as they feel it appropriate, and, as noted, they also have frequently taken the initiative to invite individuals and groups of Americans they would like to have come to China. The fact that the United States government does not extend comparable personal invitations to individual Chinese to be touring guests in this country does not in any way compromise the legitimacy of what the Chinese have been doing. One might ask whether the particular Chinese decisions have been wise or foolish, productive or counterproductive, but one cannot challenge their legality. In fairness, it must also be acknowledged that the Chinese are confronted with a problem that is not of their own making, for it is Americans who crave to go to China, and as far as we know there are few Chinese who at this time wish to visit America, or at least let it be known that they so wish. Given this lack of symmetry in interest, a lack of symmetry in policy is inevitable.

In recognizing these objective facts of Chinese legal rights and American eagerness to go to China, we must also note a third objective fact: namely, that these conditions have created some tensions among Americans. Since nobody knows the criteria the Chinese employ in granting and, more important, denying visas, an atmosphere has arisen in which all who desire to go to China feel that they must avoid doing or saying anything which they imagine might affect their prospects of getting a visa. Some scholars have felt inhibited in publicizing their views. Speculation about why some people have been granted permission and others not has affected reputations.

These inherent problems, however, take on quite a different shape when the delegations are a part of the "facilitated" exchange programs which have been agreed to by the two governments and which are supposed to be representative of the sending country. Although not "official" delegations in the sense that they can speak for either government, they are however expected to be "representative" in the sense that they are composed of people who are acknowledged specialists or authorities in the particular field of the exchange. What is special about such delegations is that they meet two criteria: (1) the two governments have in some degree mutually agreed upon the desirability of the exchange, and (2) the delegation is presumed to be representative of the sending country's professional or technical competence in the field.

It is important to keep the second distinction in mind. It is, for example, the right of the Chinese to invite whatever Americans of whatever profession they may choose, but they cannot describe such a delegation as "representing" that profession or occupation. A delegation claiming to represent a particular field in America must have the blessings of the appropriate American professional association or learned society. Granted that this distinction is often easier to make in theory than in practice, given the diffuse structure of American society, but the distinction must be maintained if there is to be smooth progress in cultural exchange.

Unfortunately, in some instances the Chinese felt it necessary to assert their legal right to deny visas to individual members of delegations which the Americans regarded as "representative" and hence the composition of which should be a matter for the sending side to decide. In the late summer of 1975 a delegation of American mayors, on the eve of their

[129]

departure for China, was presented with a Chinese decision that it would be "inconvenient" to receive the mayor of San Juan because at that time the issue of Puerto Rican independence was being bandied about in certain United Nations committees. The mayor, Carlos Romero Barcelo, was at the time the President of the National League of Cities and thus a logical member of the delegation. Faced with the Chinese decision, the sponsoring organization, the National Committee on U.S.-China Relations, and the rest of the delegation felt they had no alternative but to cancel the trip. A few years earlier a delegation of linguists was about to leave for China when Peking refused a visa for the one China specialist accompanying the group. In this case when the sponsoring organization, the Committee on Scholarly Communication with the People's Republic of China, informed Peking that the rest of the delegation would refuse to proceed to China, the Chinese relented and granted the necessary visa.

The principle that the sending country should select the members of its own delegations is the best guarantee that representativeness will be achieved. Those involved on each side in organizing delegations know more about the structure of their own societies and thus are in the better position to design truly representative groups. This does not mean that discussion between sponsoring and host organizations should not take place as planning proceeds. Indeed, after its visit a delegation might want to suggest that certain people it met be invited to visit its country. In fact, it is to be hoped that as scholars become more knowledgeable about the research going on in the other country they will develop personal contacts which should indeed be followed up on return visits.

All this leads to the principle that the sending country should select its delegation but that the receiving country may request that certain people be included. If the receiving country feels that it must excercise its sovereign rights of denying a visa to any particular individual, then the rest of the delegation should agree to cancel the visit.

RECIPROCITY AND THE PROBLEMS OF "FAIRNESS"

The lack of symmetry in interest among Chinese and Americans in the various aspects of the cultural exchange relationship has created serious issues of equity and reciprocity. While both sides have the desire to improve cultural relations, they tend to have different expectations and different constraints, and hence it is objectively hard to find formulae which would insure a sense of reciprocity. Healthy growth in cultural exchanges does require mutual respect for the interests of the other party and a recognition of the differences in needs of the two countries.

The issue of reciprocity arises because the Chinese have assumed that it is entirely natural that they should send to the United States whatever delegation or group they want, and that they should also have the right to pick and choose from among those whom the Americans want to send. The question of reciprocity also arises because the Chinese essentially decide what any American delegation will do during its visit to China, while the Chinese delegations determine for the most part what they will do while visiting America.

The problem is greatly complicated because the Chinese, thinking in terms of all the channels (from the *ad hoc* and "friendship" groups through the facilitated program), naturally assume that they have been generous in receiving Americans and thus responsive to the imbalance caused by the American craving to travel. But those Americans involved in the facilitated exchanges are sensitive to the fact that they have

[131]

only that channel and therefore tend to see the problem of reciprocity entirely in terms of satisfying mutual interest through these negotiations. At this level there is some justice in the American complaint because, as we have noted, it is only the facilitated exchanges which can advance "the spirit of the Shanghai Communiqué."

Clearly, the answer is not one of mechanical equivalence in which delegations going each way would be paired according to fields of interest. Americans and Chinese do have different ranges of interests and skills; therefore if the exchanges are to be representative of the two cultures, there will have to be differences in the nature of the delegations each side sends.

The nub of the problem is to achieve a degree of fairness in making exchanges equally responsive to the different interests of the two sides. Here is a situation in which Americans seem to be at fault in causing troubles which, ironically, bother them especially. To repeat, whereas the Chinese do seem to have a clear set of priorities among their objectives in the exchanges, the United States government, at least, does not have specific preferences beyond making its private clients of the exchanges happy. Yet when the negotiations for annual exchange "packages" end up with the Chinese interest seemingly far better fulfilled, it is the Americans who complain about reciprocity. This somewhat absurd situation arises from the fact that as long as the United States government does not have reasons for its own preferences, the problem then becomes one of satisfying all the private interests who do have a desire to participate in exchanges. And since this cannot be done because there are too many such interests, the inevitable result is frustration.

In trying to find a proper principle of reciprocity, it must be acknowledged that the Chinese have every right to seek the maximum number of exchanges in those areas in which they have the greatest interest. Yet it is to be hoped that the

Chinese will realize that their long-range political interests may be better served if they make concessions to the wider range of Americans who have special interests in exchanges. In time the Chinese may discover that short-run gains which exploit the current enthusiasm of Americans for China can cause long-range public relations problems if important segments of American society feel frustrated by the emerging trends in cultural exchange.

The Chinese, for example, are at present very eager to use cultural exchange to gain greater access to American technology. This is in itself a perfectly proper interest. The pitfall, however, is that since much of the technology which the Chinese seek falls in the domain of industry in the United States, it would thus be more appropriate for them to deal with elements of American industry than with the American scholarly community. Unfortunately for the Chinese, however, American industry does not exist to participate in cultural exchange, but rather to make profits through sales. Industrial laboratories have only a marginal interest in sharing their technological know-how, especially if it appears that there will be no sales in the offing. American academic scientists, moreover, are generally not interested in the technical engineering problems which preoccupy the Chinese.

The problem of reciprocity is exacerbated because the Chinese apparently have absolutely no interest in exchanges in precisely those areas in which there is intense American interest. Specifically, Chinese place a very low priority on cultural exchange in the fields of the humanities and in social science research, whereas in America these are precisely the fields with the longest traditions of interest in China and the largest numbers of scholars with professional concerns that make it desirable for them to travel to China and, perhaps in time, even to engage in empirical research.

Thus, it has been the Chinese who have pressed for

delegations in specific areas of advanced science and technology, such as computer and laser technology, hydraulic engineering, telecommunications, industrial automation, or in applied areas such as insect hormones, herbal pharmacology, plant photosynthesis, molecular biology, petrochemicals, and immunology. The American delegations to China have tended to have somewhat more general interest and have included broad-ranging medical delegations, physicists, child development specialists, and teachers. But in response to the Chinese interest in highly technical matters there have also been American delegations in plant studies, seismology, schistosomiasis, insect control, and computer sciences.

From 1972 through 1975 there has been a total of 59 facilitated exchanges in both directions: 40 delegations in the technical and scientific field, 9 generalist delegations (including college presidents, world affairs leaders, and the promoters of cultural exchanges), 6 athletic teams, and 4 "performing arts" groups, including the Philadelphia Orchestra.

The fact that of these 59 facilitated exchanges, 32 were Chinese groups coming to America and 27 were American groups points to another problem of reciprocity. As noted earlier, there has been much popular pressure from Americans wishing to visit China. Indeed, when all "channels" and not just the facilitated exchanges are counted, there have been about ten times as many American visitors as Chinese. Yet in the facilitated exchanges there have been more Chinese delegations, and this has caused some complications for the CSCPRC, which has received 21 Chinese delegations and sent 14. (In 1975 the Chinese sent 7 and the Americans 5.) Therefore, in preparation for the negotiations for 1976, the CSCPRC proposed that there should be an equal number of delegations each way. Its request for reciprocity ran into a Chinese policy decision to hold constant the levels of exchanges, presumably as an indication of dissatisfaction about the pace of "normalization" and American policies regarding détente and Taiwan. In this situation the "private" aspect of the CSCPRC was prepared to make a stronger stand than the State Department took, and in the face of an unbending Chinese position, the CSCPRC decided to schedule two of the seven Chinese groups in 1977 in order to achieve a balanced program in 1976 of five groups each way. By 1977, one hopes, both sides will be ready to expand the numbers, but in the meantime the CSCPRC has couragiously fought for reciprocity.

If cultural exchanges are in fact to grow, American academic scientists will have to accept that their Chinese opposite numbers are much more absorbed with applied technology than with pure science. The Chinese authorities, for their part, will need to appreciate the extent to which American social scientists and humanists can influence the intellectual environment which shapes American thinking about China, and decide not to frustrate them unduly.

There is another difference in attitudes and style which contributes to the American sense that reciprocity is absent in many of the exchange relationships. This difference arises from the American national compulsion for being "open in human relations," for "sharing one's thoughts," and for engaging in "dialogues," and the Chinese style for being correct, dignified, and reserved, if not secretive. Americans appreciate the considerations of their hosts, but they often feel that all the banqueting and toasting to friendship can become an obstacle to the free-flowing interchange of ideas and opinions, which they feel should be the goal of exchanges. The fact that Chinese officials, no matter how graciously, speak only the official line seems to surprise Americans and leave them with a feeling that the Chinese are not meeting them half-way.

This problem lies very much in the grip of national

character and thus it is not likely to disappear. It is, however, probably intensified today because on each side there are some considerations, only temporary, one hopes, which tend to exaggerate the natural inclinations. In China, political requirements do demand conformity, and those who are exposed to dealing with foreigners in exchanges must be careful to conduct themselves so that they will not become the targets of criticism of those Chinese who oppose all dealings with potential "enemies." In contrast, among Americans today the dominant mood is antigovernment, and everyone is anxious to outdo the other in displaying independence.

As we have now gone beyond the general issue of reciprocity into the substantive issues of exchange activities, it is appropriate to address the questions which surround the negotiation of agendas and schedules.

NEGOTIATIONS: AGENDAS AND PROGRAMS

The success of cultural exchange depends in large measure upon what happens once a delegation from one country arrives in the other. Chinese and Americans seem to have quite different instincts as to what are the proper subjects for the daily agendas and the total program for visiting delegations. Americans have what can only be described as a fanatical belief that it is absolutely essential for visitors to be exposed to (1) sordid scenes, and (2) the informalities of family life. When the first Chinese ping-pong team visited America, it was seen almost as a national disgrace if the Chinese were not taken into the slums or ghettos of each of the cities they visited. The appearance of a Chinese delegation in any American city also brings forth a host of invitations to private homes. The Chinese, in contrast, are convinced that regardless of the professional interests of the delegation, all foreigners will be interested in seeing factories, industrial exhibits, communes, kindergartens and, of course, ancient historical sights. Fortunately, Americans are responsive to sight-seeing and have been quick to grasp the status importance of the various routine tour sites of China. Needless to say, the Chinese feel that they can only honor their guests by showing them the best they have to offer.

This difference in national style defies ideological preference. Both conservative and radical Americans crave to show everything, while all classes of Chinese instinctively know that they should always put their best foot forward. Shirley MacLaine, in the context of visiting China, is inspired to cultural masochism, seeing only the worst in her fellow travelers and her country, but blinded to all defects in her hosts.

The Chinese art of hospitality is certainly one of the great cultural feats of the world, and it would be utterly impossible to fault the Chinese as hosts. Cultural exchanges with China have benefited greatly from the wonders of the Chinese cuisine and no one should want to eliminate the traditions of Chinese banquets, even though some Americans, as we have noted, do feel that they can become too ritualized.

The growth of cultural exchanges does require, however, that the relationship should go beyond the level of tourism and social hospitality. There is a need for genuine intellectual exchange and more opportunities for people with specialized skills to share thoughts and views with their colleagues in the other country. The objective of seeking more meaningful interaction does not have to include the rather extreme American ideal of heart-to-heart dialogues on all manner of matters. What is required is only assurance that progress is being steadily made toward procedures which will encourage greater mutual understanding.

At present the characteristic procedure for "negotiating"

[137]

the agenda or schedule of an exchange is for the visiting American negotiators to send ahead their suggestions; almost immediately after they arrive in China, there is a meeting at which the visitors' proposals are reviewed. Then comes a waiting period as higher Chinese authorities decide what in fact will take place and what is "inconvenient" or "cannot be arranged." The process is not what is usually thought of as negotiations since there is no give-and-take; yet persistence on the part of the Americans can, at times, produce some modifications.

Generally, however, most Americans are so excited about being in China that the prospect of routine sight-seeing and boiler-plate briefings becomes a form of consciousness-raising. Those fortunate enough to have audiences with the foreign minister or a vice premier invariably find proud significance in every word that was uttered as they crave to find new departures of policy and significant "signals." The mystique of China is such that all this is possible even though serious students of Chinese political behavior know that the Chinese have never communicated anything to unofficial delegations about which they have not already officially informed Washington.

In time, however, it is certain that tourism will lose its potent appeal; and if cultural exchanges are to grow in significance, it will be necessary for American and Chinese specialists in various fields to have more extended opportunities for discussion. This goal might be accomplished by having delegations stay longer in the places visited and forgo touring in favor of more intensive studies of particular problems.

Progress toward such a reasonable objective has been retarded in part by the Chinese practice of giving very precise status treatment to each American delegation, and by the remarkable alacrity with which Americans have responded to the prestige of even modest degrees of elite gradation. If a delegation senses that it is being given a specific form of V.I.P. treatment, it almost certainly reacts by counting its blessings and not doing anything which might be construed as ungracious in the eyes of its hosts.

While Americans may seem to be easily shackled by such treatment, it is in fact the Chinese who are the prisoners of a practice which requires that every delegation be given its appropriate treatment according to a clear hierarchical scale. Instead of following the easier practice of assuming that each delegation, because of its different interests, ought to be given a different program and treatment, or handling delegations on a first-come, first-serve basis or, even more shocking, according to the market principle of what they are prepared to pay— the Chinese seem to feel compelled to fit each delegation into a preconceived pattern of ranking. What seems to frustrate them is the inescapable fact that if they are to keep special treatment for a limited few they must risk offending the large majority. The Chinese instinct for hospitality is such that they seem utterly incapable of blurring status differences.

Hospitality and Political Advocacy

This brings us to what Americans sense as an anomaly in the Chinese approach to cultural exchange, and what the Chinese must feel is the proper objective of exchanges. To the American mind, hospitality is associated with kindliness, consideration for others, and gentility—qualities entirely divorced from any calculations of power and political advantage. Political advocacy is perceived as involving the aggressive assertion of self-interest and completely inappropriate to refined social relations. Therefore, the contemporary Chinese are as mystifying as the classical Chinese because they, more than any people in the world, can combine what Americans see as irreconcilable: hospitality and political advocacy. Chinese culture today is both dedicated to impressing visitors and permeated with the primacy of political considerations.

This difference in perspectives raises some awkward problems for cultural exchanges. Americans are convinced that it is utterly improper to introduce blatant political matters into the domain of cultural exchanges, which we feel should be inspired by the sentiments appropriate to hospitality and smooth interpersonal relations. For the Chinese, there must be something unnatural in separating friendship and politics.

These differences in understanding no doubt contributed to an unfortunate incident in March 1975, when the Chinese at the last minute sought to introduce into the program of an impending visit of a performing arts troupe a propagandistic song dealing with the "liberation of Taiwan." The manner in which the Chinese acted suggested that they were intent on testing the resolve of the Americans to keep cultural presentations nonpolitical. Under the circumstances, it was entirely appropriate that the National Committee on U.S.-China Relations stood firm, even to the point of having to see a long-prepared visit cancelled.

In the future, nevertheless, it is certain that the Chinese view that hospitality and political advocacy are blendable will taint cultural exchanges to some degree. This is so for no more reason than that the Chinese have so little to offer in exchanges that are not colored by their perspective on politics. Nearly all their songs and certainly all their operas, the most important "cultural" forms they have, are devoted to "revolutionary" themes.

This brings us to an awkward point: shall we assume that, just because the Chinese are such a politicized society and they may have little "culture" to offer that is not political, the United States should seek to introduce political themes into its exchanges with the Chinese?

One principle of equity would hold that both sides should either eschew explicit political themes, or introduce whatever political messages they choose. Against the argument for exclusion there is the concept that exchanges should be representative of each society, and China is certainly a completely politicized society while Americans make a point in knowing how to draw a line between partisan politics and civility. According to this reasoning it would be appropriate for the Chinese to display their "revolutionary" messages in this country while the Americans maintain their nonpolitical approach. Tolerance for the Chinese predilections will no doubt vary according to judgments of how American audiences are likely to react to even the most blatant forms of Chinese political propaganda. Let it be said that some champions of better understanding between the two countries worry that American audiences may find such Chinese "revolutionary" fare puerile. But if the Chinese are ready to risk discrediting their image as serious people, maybe others should not intervene too much in their learning process. Certainly the American theater-going population has been exposed to far more revolutionary ideas than anything Chinese society can offer.

ALTERNATIVE ARRANGEMENTS

The fact of complications in the exchange program may cause some people to wonder whether there may not be better approaches. Could we avoid the tensions associated with negotiating agendas and the search for reciprocity by dispensing with all facilitated exchanges? Have other countries hit upon happier formulae?

If the United States were to dispense with facilitated exchanges, then the field would be left to Friendship Associations and to whatever *ad hoc* programs the Chinese might be able to arrange. The Chinese would then have to meet directly all the pressures inspired by the phenomenon of "Marco Polo-itis" in America; and in satisfying some, they would inevitably antagonize many. They would have to arrive at a clear set of priorities in dealing with American society, and they could no longer treat with some elements through one channel and with others through other channels. And, of course, they would have to bear unilaterally the burden of the inevitable process of disenchantment and cynicism which follows any fashionable enthusiasm among Americans.

In addition, the abandonment of facilitated exchanges would practically bring to an end all visits to America by Chinese. Since 1972, outside of the facilitated exchange programs, only 213 Chinese have come to America. Almost all of them have been involved in business transactions—130 were technicians receiving training with Boeing aircraft and Kellogg fertilizers—and only 23 have been associated with privately arranged scientific or scholarly delegations. If there is any merit in Chinese scholars and scientists visiting this country, then it is essential to have facilitated exchanges.

The end of facilitated exchanges would also mean an end to Chinese sports teams and performing arts troupes visiting this country because such groups, in their exposure to public audiences, need the security arrangements which are only possible with facilitated exchanges.

Abandonment of facilitated exchanges would also create problems with regard to objective reporting on what is to be seen and learned in China. Once the principle of reciprocity is cast aside, then the Chinese would be free to invite only those they could confidently expect to report Chinese developments as the Chinese would like to have them reported. The process of receiving visas and being taken on standard tours could soon become completely politicized.

In some respects this is precisely what has happened with Sino-Japanese cultural exchanges. The Japanese government decided not to intervene in the exchanges, and now the only Japanese scholars able to visit China are those with recognized biases in favor of the People's Republic. Neutral and skeptical scholars, to say nothing of critical ones, have no chances to travel in China.

Britain's exchanges had almost drifted into a mold similar to the Japanese one, but increasingly London has been working to create a system not too unlike the American-Chinese one, with some facilitated exchanges. In the case of Sino-British exchanges the prime focus has not been on science and technology, but rather on mutual language training. The Chinese feel that they need a lot more teachers of English, and in return they have been willing to allow limited numbers of Englishmen to study, mainly Chinese language, for prolonged periods in China.

Canadian exchange arrangements have been at the other extreme, strongly government-to-government, with cultural attachés in the respective capitals directly negotiating and supervising most exchange arrangements. It is to be expected under these conditions, however, that cultural exchanges will fluctuate with all the changing currents of Canadian-Chinese relations. The Canadian government can strongly support the cultural program, but there is also the danger that complications in the cultural realm could unduly dampen interstate relations.

On balance, therefore, it does seem that the pattern which

has evolved in Chinese-American relations, while not without its flaws, is possibly the most serviceable one. Exchanges are sensitive to the state of political relations, but not excessively so. Governments can bring pressures, but there is also a role for autonomous American scholars. The two principal American organizations involved in the facilitated exchanges can appreciate the goals of governmental policies, but they also have their independent standards and constituencies. As private institutions with public responsibilities they can protect the interests of the American scholarly and cultural community by shielding them from the demands of either government and by depoliticizing as much as possible the exchange process. The role these organizations play makes it possible for individual American scholars and specialists to follow their professional concerns and contribute to international goodwill without being put in the compromising position of being ideological partisans.

What Does the Future Hold?

In turning attention away from the past and from the immediate problems and trying to perceive the future, it seems that cultural exchanges are now at a critical juncture. Some observers may argue with this judgment but minimize its significance on the grounds that the fate of cultural exchanges is entirely functional to the state of the political relations between the two countries. In an ultimate sense this is of course entirely correct, yet, as we observed at the outset, cultural relations are the most visible dimension of current Sino-American relations and have as well a dynamic and logic of their own. Cultural exchanges thus both reflect the state of Sino-American relations and are in themselves a basic feature of that relationship.

[144]

At present, the most troublesome prospect is that the facilitated exchanges do not have the momentum essential for healthy growth. The great danger is that the Chinese, in striving to stabilize exchanges at a modest level, will set a level which is too low to maintain the "critical mass" necessary to give life and dynamism to the organizations necessary for such exchanges. If the facilitated exchanges should seem to be frozen while the Friendship Association exchanges are expanded, the risk will be that everyone will see exchanges as essentially political activities, and Americans will increasingly see trips to China as "guided" and not just tours. Suspicions that the Chinese are indeed masking the realities of their society and propagandizing their visitors, as the Russians once did, will be strengthened if the legitimizing role of the "facilitated" exchanges is weakened. This is a gloomy prospect which, one hopes, will not come about.

If we look in the direction of possible optimistic outcomes, it is still necessary to be cautious in forecasting glowing developments. If many, or most, of the problems identified above were to be satisfactorily resolved, there could be a healthy growth in exchange relationships, but it will still not be realistic to expect easy and free-flowing give-and-take among representatives of the two societies.

It must be remembered that those Chinese who had the most extensive experiences with Westerners suffered much during the 1950s and 1960s because of suspicions about their possible loyalties. The pattern of what has happened in cultural exchanges with the Soviet Union may not be particularly relevant because in Russia there has long been a strong tradition of science and the artistic and intellectual activities of the West are well known, and therefore, by and large, the "Russianness" of Soviet scientists and intellectuals has not been so subject to challenge. In China, by contrast, because science and the modern arts were for the most part imported, their devotees have always been vulnerable to the charge of being unduly fascinated with foreign ways and not entirely loyal to Chinese ways,

It is this problem which places cultural exchanges at the very heart of the historic Chinese struggle to modernize, and which makes cultural exchanges with China something far more than just an exercise in fostering international goodwill. For 150 years the Chinese have been struggling to gain aspects of "foreign culture" while preserving their own "culture." Once the issue was between Western culture and Confucian values; now it is between a world culture of modernity and Maoist values.

As we have noted, the China of today is again confronting issues of the turn of the century when Chinese reformers preached the idea that their country could take in Western science and know-how in order to preserve the traditional Confucian values. Other, more conservative Chinese argued that it would be impossible to make such a distinction between techniques and basic values. Ironically, today it is the Chinese "radicals" who are inclined to the traditionally Chinese conservative view that the import of foreign technology can readily lead to the destruction of basic values, while the present-day "moderates" see merit in what was once the radical view.

Eventually, China must work out its "cultural" problem and come to terms with the fact that it, like all countries, must live with a blend of cosmopolitan and parochial "cultures." So far it has never been possible anywhere in the world to isolate a culture of science which is pure know-how and untainted by human values. Possibly, the Chinese will succeed in this unlikely enterprise. What is certainly clear is that they cannot become a modern society without the benefits of modern technology, which will require contacts with the rest of the world.

[146]

Cultural exchanges thus go directly to a central issue in the modernization of China, the relation of Western technology and Chinese values. But there is even more to the importance of cultural exchanges than this, for in a fundamental sense the key issue in the Chinese revolution of the last 100 years has been the question of how China should fit into the world scene. It is this issue which makes cultural exchanges a truly significant part of China's historical development. Both Confucian and Maoist China have been distinctive societies which to a unique degree have been most comfortable when in isolation. But the world is now such that one-quarter of humanity cannot withdraw into itself. How the Chinese meet the various tests inherent in the cultural exchange process will foreshadow much of their prospects for national development.

Fortunately, cultural exchanges are also a two-way proposition so that others can be involved in China's real revolution. The question for Americans is how they can help China without being either patronizing or sycophantic. In part, the answer involves building a stronger cultural exchange relationship so that eventually the "cultural" problem with respect to China will become the same as that with all other countries, namely, the expansion of goodwill and understanding. Today it would be fatuous to focus only on goodwill and to ignore the great issues of how China is to absorb modern technology and become more effectively integrated into an interdependent world. At the same time it would provoke the old Chinese fears of foreign exploitation to concentrate only on the technological and political dimensions of the problem and ignore the importance of goodwill. The great virtue of facilitated cultural exchanges is that they provide a unique opportunity to blend problem-solving and goodwill.

NOTES

1. For a general account of the development of cultural exchanges see: Douglas P. Murray, "Exchanges with the People's Republic of China: Symbols and Substance," *The Annals,* Vol. 424 (March 1976), pp. 29-42.

2. According to the estimate of the CSCPRC, the American scholars visiting China represented the following fields. The figures in parentheses give the number of scholars on facilitated exchanges.

	Subtotals by disciplines		Totals	
Agricultural Sciences			26	(2)
Atmospheric and Earth Sciences			21	(4)
Engineering			65	(34)
Mathematics and Physical Sciences			97	(47)
Mathematics	14	(9)		
Chemistry	12	(7)		
Physics	71	(31)		
Bio-Medical Sciences			139	(28)
Biology	29			
Medical	110			
Social Sciences and Humanities			313	(48)
Humanities	82			
Social Sciences	231			
TOTAL			661	(163)

3. Donald Munro, Chapter 2, "The Concept of Mind," in *The Concept of Man in Contemporary China* (Ann Arbor: University of Michigan Press, forthcoming).

4. Murray, *op. cit.*, pp. 32-33.

[148]

[FIVE]

The Taiwan Issue in Sino-American Relations *

Ralph N. Clough

The Shanghai Communiqué of February 27, 1972, was interpreted by many at the time, especially in Japan, as pointing the way to an early resolution of the Taiwan problem through negotiations between Peking and Taipei that would lead to the integration of Taiwan with mainland China.[1] The United States declared (1) that it did not challenge the view held by Chinese on both sides of the Taiwan strait that Taiwan was part of China; (2) that it reaffirmed its interest in peaceful settlement of the Taiwan question by the Chinese themselves; and (3) that it intended to withdraw all its forces and military installations from the island. Although by this statement the United States virtually disavowed any interest in an independent Taiwan and tipped the scale toward a

* This chapter is based on a forthcoming study of Taiwan and U.S.-China policy, sponsored by the Twentieth Century Fund.

negotiated settlement of the prolonged Chinese civil war, the declaration fell far short of resolving the Taiwan problem.

Today, more than five years later, the United States has not yet established full diplomatic relations with the Peoples' Republic of China (PRC). It continues to maintain a security treaty with the Republic of China (ROC) on Taiwan as well as extensive economic and other relations. Although it has withdrawn most of its military forces from the island, some 1,400 U.S. military personnel remain. And the government of the ROC shows no signs of willingness to negotiate with the PRC or to take any other action that would weaken its ability to remain free of the mainland's control. On the contrary, in its long-term planning Taiwan envisages further strengthening of its economic and defense capabilities and further enlargement of its already extensive economic relations with many countries throughout the world. Thus, Taiwan remains an unresolved issue between the United States and the PRC, although the Chinese, more concerned about the Soviet threat to their interests than the early "liberation" of Taiwan, have not pressed hard for a resolution of the issue.

Even if the United States were to break relations with Taiwan and establish full diplomatic relations with the PRC, there is little reason to expect that this act would lead to the early peaceful resolution of the Taiwan question by the Chinese themselves. Much will depend upon the perceptions that the United States, China, and Japan will have of their interests in Taiwan in relation to other possibly more important interests. In turn, their moves will be influenced by the policies adopted by Taiwan itself. Only after analyzing these factors and the indirect influence of the U.S.S.R. can the longer-term policy alternatives be realistically evaluated.

U.S. Interests in Taiwan: Shifting Perceptions

The most remarkable feature of the interests of the United States in Taiwan is the way that perceptions of them have ballooned or shrunk over time in the eyes of its policy makers. U.S. policy toward Taiwan has not grown out of some intrinsic interest in the island, but has been subsidiary to broader U.S. objectives in the Pacific. In this respect, the commitment to Taiwan is quite unlike the commitment to Israel. Not only was the "China lobby" never comparable to the "Israel lobby" in political influence, but Taiwan never had the symbolic significance for Americans that Israel acquired as a homeland for a historically persecuted people.

Taiwan first attracted the attention of Americans in the nineteenth century as an unhealthy, badly ruled territory where wrecked American ships were plundered and their crews mistreated or killed. Neither protests to the imperial government in Peking nor punitive expeditions by the United States and other maritime powers put an end to these perils to commerce. American officials in East Asia, including Commodore Perry, Commissioner Peter Parker in China, and Townsend Harris, the first American envoy to Japan, recommended that the United States seek to acquire Taiwan by one means or another, but Washington showed no interest. When the Japanese took Taiwan from China in 1895 as a result of the Sino-Japanese War, not only was there no opposition from the U.S. government to the move, but probably a general feeling of satisfaction that an effective government had assumed responsibility for that troublesome island.

Taiwan assumed a totally different aspect for the United States in 1941, however, when it became the base for the

Japanese attack on the Philippines and advance into Southeast Asia; postwar interests seemed then to demand that the strategic island be taken out of Japanese hands. Consequently, President Franklin D. Roosevelt agreed at Cairo in November 1943 with Winston Churchill and Chiang Kai-shek that Taiwan should be returned to China. Roosevelt's main concern at the time seemed to be the need to bolster Chinese resistance to the advancing Japanese. Neither he nor senior American officials seem to have considered the possibility either of annexing Taiwan or of offering its inhabitants the choice of independence. Nor did the United States intervene after the Chinese took over the island when the Taiwanese uprising of February-March 1947 was bloodily suppressed. Relations between Taiwan and the mainland were regarded by American officials as entirely a Chinese affair.

After the collapse of Chinese Nationalist resistance on the mainland and the removal of the government of the Republic of China to Taiwan, the U.S. government decided to withdraw from any further involvement in the Chinese civil war, despite demands by prominent Republican members of Congress for further aid to the beleaguered forces of Chiang Kai-shek. President Truman announced in January 1950:

> the United States has no desire to obtain special rights or privileges or to establish military bases in Formosa at this time. Nor does it have any intention of utilizing its armed forces to interfere in the present situation. The United States Government will not pursue a course which will lead to involvement in the civil conflict in China. Similarly, the United States Government will not provide military aid or advice to Chinese forces on Formosa.[2]

Chiang Kai-shek and his forces were thus left to fend for themselves.

[152]

But with the outbreak of the Korean war in June 1950, the United States altered its evaluation of its interests in Taiwan overnight. President Truman declared:

the occupation of Formosa by Communist forces would be a direct threat to the security of the Pacific area and to United States forces performing their lawful and necessary functions in that area. Accordingly, I have ordered the Seventh Fleet to prevent any attack on Formosa. . . . The determination of the future status of Formosa must await the restoration of security in the Pacific, a peace settlement with Japan, or consideration by the United Nations.[3]

Thereafter, the United States resumed its programs of economic and military aid to the Republic of China, expanding them rapidly after Peking's forces intervened in Korea. American missionaries, denied entry to mainland China, turned their attention to Taiwan. Links between the United States and Taiwan proliferated. A bilateral security treaty signed in December 1954 added to the chain of alliances being forged by Secretary of State John Foster Dulles in his efforts to contain the spread of communism. Taiwan came to be regarded as a key strategic link in the U.S. policy of containment.

During the 1960s, however, perceptions of U.S. national interests in relations with Taiwan underwent further modification. The growing conflict between China and the Soviet Union, the erosion of support for the Republic of China's position in the United Nations, and the impact of the Vietnam war caused gradual changes in public attitudes. Thus, President Nixon's opening to China was widely acclaimed. Few criticized the revised definition of U.S. interests in Taiwan that the Shanghai Communiqué implied. Although the language of the communiqué was ambiguous in some respects, leaving unclear the timing and tactics of future U.S. policy toward Peking and Taipei, one fact was obvious: The United States had quietly abandoned the view of Taiwan as a critical strategic position for checking the expansion of Peking's power and influence.

It is evident that this modified view of U.S. interests arose not out of changes in Taiwan itself or in American relations with Taiwan, but rather out of changes in the U.S. perception of the PRC. President Nixon perceived that the hostile, sterile confrontation between Washington and Peking which had prevailed for so many years did not serve national interests in the circumstances of the 1970s. Peking, now confronted by a hostile Soviet Union, was not in a position to pose a military threat to its neighbors. The opening of relations with Peking, as Washington saw it, would improve prospects for creating an enduring equilibrium of power in East Asia and would strengthen the U.S. negotiating position vis-à-vis the U.S.S.R. For its own reasons, the PRC wanted improved relations with the United States. Consequently, Washington and Peking were able to devise a formula for putting aside the Taiwan issue, which for so long had blocked any improvement in their bilateral relations. The issue, though still unresolved, was now regarded by both parties to the Shanghai Communiqué as less important than the broader interests which they sought to promote by fostering relations with each other.

Although the United States had agreed with the PRC to put aside the Taiwan issue for the time being, it continued to have an important interest in the way that issue is ultimately resolved. It is not possible to turn history back 25 years and resume an attitude of indifference to the fate of the people on Taiwan. Bonds that have been created between Taiwan and the United States over this period, including a solemn defense commitment made by the President with the advice and consent of the U.S. Senate, cannot be ignored. Nor can Americans be oblivious to the right to self-determination of a numerous people who clearly are capable and desirous of conducting their own affairs. U.S. economic interests in Taiwan are relatively small, but not negligible. Two-way trade in 1975 reached $3.5 billion, as compared with trade of $463 million between the United States and the PRC. Investments by American firms totaled close to $375 million, while Export-Import Bank loans amounted to $1.2 billion, and guarantees to an additional $700 million.[4]

While the improvement in U.S. relations with the PRC has been almost universally applauded, total severance of relations with Taiwan would be strongly opposed.[5] Many Americans would argue that it would be wrong on both moral and political grounds for the United States to abandon the people of Taiwan to possible military conquest by the PRC. Consequently, the problem facing the U.S. government is how to reconcile its broad interest in developing a constructive relationship with the PRC with a continuing, even though subsidiary, interest in the future of the people of Taiwan.

PRC INTERESTS IN TAIWAN: TERRA IRREDENTA

The interests of the People's Republic of China in Taiwan are obviously more deep-rooted and potentially more important than those of the United States. Few issues can stir nationalistic emotions so readily as territorial claims. Taiwan resembles Hong Kong and Macao in being a piece of territory inhabited by Chinese, politically once part of but now separated from the homeland. With its rapidly industrializing economy and its skilled and literate population, Taiwan is an

[155]

increasingly attractive economic prize for the PRC, if it could be recovered at reasonable cost. It is not, like Hong Kong, insulated against takeover by making a vital contribution to the PRC's balance of payments.

For many years Taiwan posed a serious political threat and, to a lesser extent, a military threat to the PRC. It was the home of a rival government which proclaimed as its basic policy the overthrow of the PRC and contested the latter's legitimacy in the international community. The armed forces of the Republic of China, if provided with large quantities of logistic support by the United States, were capable of giving effective support to any large-scale dissident movement opposed to the central government that might arise in South China.

The PRC's willingness to put aside the Taiwan issue temporarily in order to improve relations with the United States arose in part from its concern with the Soviet threat and from its desire to improve relations with Japan. These broader international concerns took precedence over Peking's interest in resolving the Taiwan issue. But the PRC hoped at the same time that by improving relations with the United States it could, in the short run, diminish the threat Taiwan posed to its interests and, in the longer run, facilitate the recovery of Taiwan.

The PRC's short-run objectives have been largely achieved. Taipei's ability to contest the legitimacy of the PRC in the international community has become negligible since the Republic of China was expelled from the United Nations and many other official and private international organizations. It now has diplomatic relations with only 24 countries, a trend toward diplomatic isolation which seems irreversible. Moreover, the decision by the United States to seek improved relations with the PRC virtually eliminated any significant military threat from Taiwan to the mainland.

The PRC, like the United States, faces a dilemma in shaping its future policy toward Taiwan. So long as it gives a high priority to strengthening its position relative to the U.S.S.R.—"uniting all that can be united" to oppose the principal enemy—it cannot afford to push the Taiwan issue to the point where it becomes a serious impediment to competing with the Soviet Union for influence on the United States and Japan. Moreover, Peking must concern itself with trends on Taiwan itself. It has an important stake in the view espoused by Taiwan's leaders at present that the island is part of China. Excessive pressure might force Taiwan's present or future leadership to declare in desperation the island's independence or even—Peking's worst nightmare—to seek backing from the Soviet Union. The PRC's problem, then, is to devise a combination of inducements and pressures directed at the United States, Japan, and Taiwan itself, which will gradually but inexorably bring the island under mainland control without unduly interfering with the more important objective of strengthening its position relative to the U.S.S.R.

JAPAN'S INTERESTS IN TAIWAN: TRADE AND HISTORY

The Japanese have three types of interests in Taiwan: those growing out of Japan's historical association with the island, economic interests, and strategic concerns. Japan's 50 years as colonial ruler of Taiwan has given the Japanese a special feeling for the territory and its inhabitants unlike their feeling for any other place except Korea. Moreover, the nostalgia with which Japanese regard Taiwan is not marred by the mutual suspicion and resentment that affect Japanese-Korean relations. Significant numbers of Japanese businessmen and government officials grew up on Taiwan, went to school there or worked there, developing close personal ties with Taiwanese.

[157]

Many influential Taiwanese received their higher education in Japan, and some 4,000 students from Taiwan are in Japan today. Many of the 50,000 Chinese residents of Japan are Taiwanese, who maintain close family and other connections in Taiwan.

Economic relations between Japan and Taiwan are important and have expanded substantially since the severance of diplomatic relations in September 1972. Two-way trade in 1975 was over $2.6 billion.[6] Japanese investments in Taiwan are estimated at over $200 million.[7] In 1974, 4,000 Japanese lived in Taiwan and 439,000 visited the island.[8]

Little is said publicly about Japan's strategic interest in Taiwan, although in the 1969 Nixon-Sato communiqué Prime Minister Sato declared that security in the Taiwan area was a most important factor for the security of Japan. Privately many Japanese politicians and writers on international affairs acknowledge that Taiwan, lying close to the Ryukyu island chain and Japan's vital trade routes to Southeast Asia and the Middle East, could be a serious strategic threat in hostile hands.

In the light of these varied and important interests, many Japanese are ambivalent concerning Taiwan. There is little dissent from the view that, in the long run, Japan's relations with the PRC outweigh the importance of those with Taiwan. Consequently, the decision by Prime Minister Tanaka to establish diplomatic relations with Peking at the cost of breaking those with Taipei was almost universally supported at the time—but only because it was believed that a valuable relationship with Taiwan also could continue to exist. Foreign Minister Ohira, on his return from Peking in September 1972, expressed the Japanese view succinctly: "There are strong and deep ties between Japan and Taiwan. Consequently, even if diplomatic relations are severed, administrative relations must be respected and treasured. So long as they do not touch upon the very roots of the maintenance of Japan-China relations, we intend to devote utmost efforts for the maintenance of administrative relations between Taiwan and Japan." [9]

Because of the strong attachment to Taiwan that persists in Japan, especially among Liberal Democratic Party politicians, [10] Japanese policy toward Taiwan has frequently become a political issue. Pro-Taiwan members of the Diet severely criticized Prime Minister Tanaka for having been too hasty in establishing diplomatic relations with Peking and delayed for more than a year the conclusion of the aviation agreement with the PRC. Consequently, although the majority of Japanese would opt for good relations with the PRC over good relations with Taiwan, the pro-Taiwan lobby has considerable clout. The present situation suits Japan very well. The Japanese ruling group would not be unhappy if the United States were to continue to delay shifting diplomatic relations from Taipei to Peking so that they would not have to cope with the uncertainties which that action would create for future Japanese relations with Taiwan. The Japanese government expects the future of Taiwan to be decided by the United States and the PRC, not by Japan. It adjusts its policies so as best to serve Japanese interests in the light of the action taken by the two more directly concerned nations.

TAIWAN: A MODERNIZING SOCIETY UNDER SIEGE

With only 16 million people, the small island of Taiwan appears at the mercy of the giant powers on whose actions its security and well-being heavily depend. Yet it is evident that the giants do not have a free hand in dealing with Taiwan, being constrained in various ways by their objectives toward each other and by domestic political concerns. Consequently, Taiwan has greater scope for maneuver than might at first appear. It is, after all, a well-organized political entity with a population larger than those of two-thirds of the members of the United Nations and producing a national income equivalent to that of Israel. It has a large, fairly well equipped military force and is separated by 90 miles of frequently rough water from its only enemy. It has an impressive record of economic growth and political stability over a 25-year period.

To what extent does Taiwan's past experience furnish a guide to its future in radically different international circumstances? How vulnerable is Taiwan's political and economic system to actions by Peking, Washington, or Tokyo? Are there hidden internal weaknesses which will become apparent as Taiwan is compelled to adjust to a harsher international environment? What options are open to the island's leaders, and how would their choice affect its relations with the United States, Japan, and the China mainland?

Economic Strengths and Weaknesses

Many of the assets that contributed to Taiwan's remarkably rapid economic growth will be relatively little affected by external changes: fertile farmland making Taiwan 88 percent self-sufficient in foodstuffs; a declining population growth rate, now down to 1.8 percent annually; a literate and increasingly highly educated population; a large and growing skilled workforce; a large corps of managers in private business and government dedicated to, and experienced in, promoting economic growth; a demonstrated ability to accumulate savings, amounting to 20-30 percent of national income (as compared to 8-10 percent in the United States); widespread experience of gaining increasing material benefits from hard work; and a fairly even distribution of income.[11]

Taiwan is well launched on an ambitious program, begun in 1972, to complete ten major construction projects by the early 1980s. This program, which calls for the investment of $6 billion in five years, is intended to place Taiwan within reach of becoming a developed nation. It includes two large nuclear power plants, an integrated steel mill, a petrochemical complex, a large shipyard, and extensive improvements in port and airport facilities, highways, and railways.

But Taiwan's prosperity and ultimately its political stability are vulnerable to external developments beyond its control. Its export of goods and services amounted to 44 percent of its gross domestic product in 1974. Moreover, more than half of its foreign trade has been with its two principal trading partners, the United States and Japan. Trade with the next largest trading partner comes to less than 7 percent of total trade. Taiwan's vulnerability was demonstrated during the worldwide recession of 1974-75. Consumer prices, which had been increasing annually at a moderate 6-7 percent, shot up nearly 40 percent in 1974. Herculean government measures brought the price increase in 1975 down to about 6 percent, but economic growth slowed to a crawl. Instead of the 10 percent annual increase in GNP that had prevailed during most of the 1960s and early 1970s, GNP growth in 1974 was 0.8 percent and in 1975, 2.8 percent. In 1975, for the first time in many years the value of Taiwan's exports declined.

The government was able to soften the impact of the recession, however, by expenditures on the ten big construction projects, drawing on the budget surplus accumulated during previous years of conservative fiscal management. Although some export industries in the private sector were hard hit and had to dismiss workers, relatively few employees in the government sector—which produces 20 percent of the gross domestic product—lost their jobs. The strength of the agricultural economy and the ability of farm families to support members who lost factory jobs also helped ease the blow.

Thus, Taiwan has demonstrated an ability to weather a serious recession. The question remains, however, what would be the effect on the economy if the United States were to shift its diplomatic relations from Taipei to Peking? Would uncertainty regarding the future sharply diminish the propensity to save and cause a flight of capital? Would Taiwan's access to foreign markets, raw materials, and technology be restricted? Much would depend upon the posture of the U.S. government at the time it shifted diplomatic relations. If it indicated it expected economic relations between Taiwan and the United States to be gradually phased out, the blow to Taiwan's economy would be serious. If, on the other hand, the U.S. government convincingly showed that it envisaged the continued existence of extensive economic relations between Taiwan and the United States and encouraged further investments by Americans in Taiwan, the shock of the shift in diplomatic relations probably could be absorbed without serious economic damage.

What of the longer-range future? Taiwan has shown a ability to absorb without lasting damage to its economy, political shocks, such as the sudden change in U.S. policy toward Peking and the loss of its seat in the United Nations, and the economic shock of world recession. It is in a better position than many resource-poor developing countries to benefit from world economic recovery and expanded world trade, even without diplomatic relations with most of its trade partners. In recent years it has not been heavily dependent on a net inflow of foreign capital to sustain investment and economic growth, although it has benefited from the technological advances introduced through foreign direct investment. It also benefited from temporary access to foreign loans in order to tide over the severe blow to its balance of trade suffered in 1974 owing to the rapid rise in oil prices and the world recession.[12] The future availability to Taiwan of direct investment and loans will continue to be important to Taiwan's economic progress, for during the next ten years it will have to depend increasingly on capital-intensive and technology-intensive industries rather than the labor-intensive industries that led its economic growth during the 1960s. These new industries will require not only an infusion of advanced technology from abroad, but also, in many cases, larger amounts of capital than can be accumulated locally for single projects. Whether the needed foreign capital will be forthcoming will depend heavily, as indicated above, on the policy of the United States.

Political Strengths and Weaknesses

Taiwan's rapid economic development has been made possible by a political stability exceptional among developing nations. What are the prospects for this stability to endure under radically changed international conditions?

Taiwan's political stability during the past 25 years rested on an authoritarian single-party system under one leader, the legitimacy of whose rule was widely accepted. The ruling party, the Kuomintang (KMT), maintained its grip on power by monopolizing access to the political system. Two minor parties existed, but played no significant role; the organization of any real opposition was firmly prevented. The top KMT leaders, particularly Chiang Kai-shek himself, controlled ap-

[163]

pointments to key positions in the government bureaucracy and the armed forces. An elaborate security apparatus, operating under conditions of martial law, further safeguarded the positions of those in power.

But KMT rule was not based on coercion alone. The majority of the people enjoyed direct benefits from the system, mainly through the land reform of the early 1950s or through the higher living standards made possible by rapid economic growth, which provided better-paying jobs, increased education, better health facilities, new opportunities for businessmen, openings in the civil service, important improvements in the treatment of the military, and other requisites for a better life.

Furthermore, the KMT has permitted popular participation in the political process to an extent not known under Japanese rule. Elections have been held regularly for the provincial assembly and for county and city officials. Although those elected to provincial and local positions have limited powers and the elections are dominated by the KMT, the need for the party organization to put forward candidates who can be elected in competition with independents has subjected the election process to considerable popular influence.

The structure of the national government in Taiwan was created on the mainland in the late 1940s and transferred unchanged to Taiwan. Consequently, the National Assembly, which elects the President, the Legislative Yuan, which enacts the laws, and the Control Yuan, which inspects the bureaucracy, are all composed principally of delegates elected nearly 30 years ago. Only a few new members have been added in recent years by elections in Taiwan. So long as the government in Taipei claims to be the rightful government of China, it must maintain a political structure representing all provinces.

The main repository of political power in Taiwan is not

these elective bodies, however, nor is it the Kuomintang party organization. Power is mainly in the hands of the leading figures of the civilian and military bureaucracy, headed by Chiang Kai-shek until his death in 1975, and now by his son, Chiang Ching-kuo. The leadership presides over an increasingly complex society, balancing pressures from a great variety of interest groups. Although Chiang Ching-kuo is the most influential single figure, he must rely heavily on the views of the technocrats who contribute to the formulation of policy and supervise its execution. The ranks of the top echelons of the technocrats are continually replenished by the promotion of younger men. For example, when Chiang Ching-kuo formed his first cabinet in 1972, he replaced 9 of the 13 holders of substantive posts and the average age of ministers declined from 65 to 61. The chief of the general staff and the heads of the military services are replaced regularly every two to three years. The ruling group in Taiwan is predominantly civilian. Although the military have strong influence, they are a highly professional force and have not taken over civilian political functions as have the military in some other Asian countries.

Taiwan is, therefore, governed by a firmly established, well-trained bureaucracy under a strong leader. The process of decision-making and the machinery of government is unlikely to be severely disrupted by most conceivable external shocks. The present leader, however, is 66 years old and if he were to die within the next few years, it would probably be difficult to reach a consensus on a successor, as no obvious choice is in sight and the political system lacks an institutionalized means of replacing the top leader. Sharp disagreement within the leadership over the succession could weaken Taiwan's political system and make it more vulnerable to outside shocks and pressures.

The sharpening of differences between the 2 million recent

immigrants from China who have dominated the government since World War II and the 14 million native Taiwanese would also threaten stability. (The ancestors of the native Taiwanese—except for some 277,000 aborigines of Malay stock—came from Fukien and Kwangtung provinces on the mainland.) But this danger has clearly declined as a result of the change in American policy toward Peking. The increased need for unity in the face of growing external perils has drawn the two groups together. Their full integration is still far off, but 30 years of public education in the Mandarin dialect has facilitated intercourse and created a shared outlook on most issues. Chiang Ching-kuo has made noticeable efforts to place more Taiwanese in high government positions; many Taiwanese want faster progress in this regard, but appreciate Chiang's efforts. Any suspicion of responsiveness among mainlander leaders to offers from Peking could also create a serious rift with the Taiwanese, who would fear a "sell-out," but there is no sign of any move in this direction as mainlander leaders have their own reasons to treat overtures from Peking with suspicion.

Perhaps the greatest threat to political stability in Taiwan would arise if a widespread belief developed among the Taiwanese that the United States and Japan intended to cut ties with the island. Security measures would probably be tightened to the point where they interfered with the effectiveness of the free enterprise system. The government would probably also feel it necessary to clamp down on the safety valves which now serve to prevent the build-up of dangerous political pressures, such as the relative freedom to criticize the government in election campaigns and in the press, the liberal attitude toward travel abroad, and the siphoning-off of a sizable portion of Taiwan's college graduates to study in the United States. A sense of heightened threat from the PRC probably would make the public more willing to tolerate tighter security measures, but if overdone they could lead to rising public dissatisfaction and greater vulnerability to inducements or pressures from the PRC.

Military Strengths and Weaknesses

The 600,000 soldiers of Chiang Kai-shek's forces that were withdrawn from the mainland to Taiwan in 1949 seemed a weak shield against an assault by Mao Tse-tung's victorious legions. They were ragged, underfed, poorly equipped, and many of them were old, ill, and barefoot. Yet even against such forces an amphibious attack was no simple matter, as was demonstrated at Quemoy in October 1949 when a large-scale Communist assault was thrown back with heavy losses.

Chinese intervention in Korea triggered the resumption of U.S. military aid to Nationalist forces, and for the next 25 years American equipment, training, and advice poured into Taiwan. Through fiscal year 1974, U.S. grants and loans for military purposes amounted to $3.5 billion. The aid was primarily designed for defense, but a small capability for offensive action was also built into the program. It served in part, especially in the early years, as a morale-sustainer for homesick mainlanders who longed to recover their homeland; but the expansion of the marine corps and the supply of landing craft were also justified as necessary to ensure the resupply of the offshore islands, the retention of which served both defensive and potential offensive purposes.

Reorganized and modernized, Taiwan's army, navy, and airforce today number in all about 500,000 men with over 1,000,000 trained reserves.[13] The universal military service and retirement systems adopted in the 1950s have created a

[167]

young, fit, well-trained force. It is supplied with relatively modern aircraft, tanks, artillery, destroyers, Nike-Hercules and Hawk missiles, a radar network, and much other equipment. Although most of the weapons are not the latest models, the forces possess the firepower and the ability to use it that would enable them to put up a stout resistance.

Furthermore, Taiwan could substantially strengthen its military position by withdrawing most of its garrison forces from the offshore islands. Deployment of one-third of its ground forces to those exposed positions might invite the PRC to cut their supply lines as a means of striking a severe blow at morale in Taiwan. The Republic of China could not, as in 1958, rely on the threat of intervention by U.S. forces to deter Peking. Large reductions in the forces on Quemoy and Matsu would enable the ROC to preserve its air and naval forces for the vital task of defending Taiwan itself, rather than risk squandering them in a vain attempt to maintain lines of communication to the offshore islands. This adjustment of Taipei's military posture would not only remove the danger that Peking could inflict heavy military losses in a conflict over the offshore islands, but would also be seen by Peking as a sign of Taipei's readiness to declare independence if it lost the islands. Thus, reducing the garrisons on the offshore islands might, paradoxically, decrease the danger of an attack on them, so long as the ROC maintained its formal commitment to the "one-China" policy.

Taiwan has a growing capability to produce its own military equipment. It manufactures M-14 rifles, machine guns, mortars, small arms and artillery ammunition, and a wide variety of other military items, and it overhauls and maintains naval ships and aircraft. Under co-production arrangements, helicopters and F-5E fighters are assembled in Taiwan. For replacement of major weapons, however, and for crucial components of the helicopters and F-5's, Taiwan still depends on the United States. Its military equipment would deteriorate rapidly if denied access to spare parts from the United States, and its principal weapons systems would become obsolete in time if they could not be replaced.

Protected by the mutual defense treaty with the United States, the Republic of China has been able to reduce gradually the proportion of its rapidly rising GNP devoted to defense. In 1974 the military budget amounted to 7 percent of GNP, or about $800 million. This is a moderate expenditure for an embattled nation. Israel's military budget in 1974 amounted to about 30 percent of GNP and Egypt's to nearly 20 percent.[14] Consequently, if the mutual defense treaty were terminated and Taiwan felt more immediately threatened by military attack, it could divert additional resources to military expenditures, although at the expense of the standard of living and investment in economic growth.

Should it decide to do so, Taiwan probably could produce nuclear weapons within five to ten years as a deterrent to a PRC attack. Nuclear research has been underway on the island since 1961, and since 1973 the Republic of China has been operating a Canadian "heavy water" research reactor almost identical to the one which made possible the Indian nuclear explosion. The large American power reactors now under construction in Taiwan will produce larger amounts of plutonium than the Canadian reactor, but of a quality less suitable for weapons. Unlike India, the Republic of China signed and ratified the nuclear non-proliferation treaty; and its nuclear facilities are inspected by the International Atomic Energy Agency (IAEA), despite the expulsion of the ROC from the IAEA. In September 1975 Chiang Ching-kuo declared: "We have both the facilities and the capability to make nuclear weapons and actually considered to build up a nuclear arsenal last year; but when I broached the idea to the late president, he rejected it flatly on the ground that we cannot use nuclear weapons to hurt our own countrymen." [15]

A comparison of Taiwan's military strength with that of the PRC shows the latter to be far stronger, with a regular army six times as large as Taiwan's, 15 times as many first-line fighter aircraft, 25 times as many submarines, and far more artillery pieces, tanks, and assorted naval craft. Moreover, the PRC has nuclear weapons and bombers, which Taiwan lacks.[16] The PRC could devastate the island with nuclear weapons, but by resorting to their first use it would incur extraordinarily high long-term costs and risks in order to acquire Taiwan in a blasted and radioactive state.

In a conflict involving conventional forces, the comparative size of the total forces on each side has little bearing on the ability of the ROC to defend Taiwan. The outcome would be determined not by the much larger ground forces possessed by the PRC, but by the number it could land and supply over 90 miles or more of ocean. Although the PRC probably could eventually gain control of the sea and air around Taiwan by being willing to take heavy losses in ships and aircraft, it lacks the specialized landing craft which would enable it to build up and extend beachheads by rapid landing of tanks and artillery. It would be no easy task to invade and occupy Taiwan against determined resistance by the ROC's ground forces. Moreover, the losses suffered, expecially in aircraft, would significantly weaken the PRC's defenses against the Soviet Union.

Thus, Taiwan's present military capability to resist a PRC attack is not insignificant, even without American participation in its defense, and its capability will grow in the years to come as its industrial base expands and its ability to divert resources to military purposes increases.

THE PEKING-TAIPEI CONFRONTATION

Since 1950 the leaders of the People's Republic of China have regarded the intervention by the United States in the Chinese civil war as the prime obstacle to bringing Taiwan under their control. The United States showed its hostility toward the government of the PRC not only by promoting and aiding a regime sworn to overthrow it, but also by using American political influence throughout the world to exclude it from the United Nations and other international organizations. In the offshore island crisis of 1958 the United States demonstrated convincingly that it was prepared to intervene militarily to prevent Taiwan or even the principal offshore islands from being conquered by the PRC. That experience, together with the deepening conflict with the U.S.S.R. on other grounds, showed that the Soviet Union would not assume any serious risk of conflict with the United States in order to back up the PRC's efforts to recover Taiwan. Lacking the military force to challenge the United States on its own, the PRC was compelled to bide its time.

Efforts by the PRC to influence Taiwan directly bore little fruit. ROC security measures prevented the establishment of a pro-Peking opposition movement. Radio broadcasts directed to Taiwan and the offshore islands failed to create perceptible pro-PRC sentiment. Appeals to leading officials in Taiwan from former colleagues holding government positions on the mainland were ineffective. Chiang Kai-shek himself was adamantly opposed to any compromise or even to serious dialogue with Peking. Hence, invitations to the nationalist refugees in Taiwan to visit their homeland and offers by Chou En-lai to give Chiang a high position in the PRC fell on deaf ears.

The Taiwanese were even more difficult to influence, for they lacked the close ties with the mainland possessed by the mainlanders. The principal anti-Kuomintang political movement among Taiwanese living outside the island advocated independence for Taiwan, which was anathema to Peking. Consequently, particularly after 1958, PRC leaders recognized the importance of the fact that Chiang Kai-shek and other ROC leaders held in common with them the view that Taiwan was an inseparable part of China and strongly opposed the Taiwan independence movement. They launched no more major assaults on the offshore islands, for these islands formed a significant symbolic link between Taiwan and the mainland— to sever their connection with Taiwan might give impetus to the movement for Taiwan independence. Strident propaganda attacks on the alleged intention of the United States to create "two Chinas" or "one China and one Taiwan" betrayed PRC anxiety that American goals might indeed lie in this direction.

Although Chiang Kai-shek and his supporters never abandoned recovery of the mainland as the declared national goal of the ROC, the expectation that it could be achieved declined as the government of the PRC consolidated its position internally and gained recognition internationally. Small-scale raids against the mainland, conducted from time to time by special forces mainly to collect intelligence and sustain morale, demonstrated the formidable nature of PRC defenses. Hope for the outbreak of widespread opposition to the PRC on the mainland rose during the serious difficulties experienced after the failure of the Great Leap Forward program for economic development, causing ROC military preparations to exploit possible uprisings. But after the spring of 1962 government policy focused on the development of Taiwan, and military strategy came to concentrate almost exclusively on defense.

Both the PRC and the ROC recognize that the status of Taiwan has depended on the nature of the U.S. connection with the island. For the past 25 years Taiwan has relied heavily on the United States—for the deterrence of military attack from the mainland, for economic and military aid, for the support of its international position, and as a market and source of capital and technology. The significance of the Shanghai Communiqué to both Chinese governments was its signal of a change in the U.S. connection. The timing and modalities of change were unclear, but the direction was unmistakable. Consequently, since 1971 the policy of the PRC has been to press the United States, mildly but persistently, to loosen its connection with Taiwan, concentrating first on diplomatic relations, the defense commitment, and the remaining resident U.S. military personnel. The PRC has also stepped up its efforts to isolate Taiwan diplomatically and have it expelled from all types of international organizations. Taiwan has reacted by working to retain a strong connection with the United States, to delay the shift of U.S. diplomatic relations to Peking as long as possible, and to adjust to the erosion of its diplomatic relations elsewhere by establishing other forms of representation abroad.

Toward Taiwan itself, the PRC has launched an extensive campaign to improve the prospects for its eventual incorporation into China. The most authoritative exposition of the PRC position was in a five-hour interview given by Chou En-lai to a group of overseas Chinese in August 1972. Chou said patience was called for, as the "liberation" of Taiwan was a very complex matter. A military solution should be avoided. The PRC was willing to negotiate with the present regime, but that regime would have to be replaced. Living standards in Taiwan would not be lowered by its incorporation into China.

[173]

Chou invited Taiwanese to visit the mainland to learn about China, and he emphasized the importance of the role of Taiwanese in the "liberation." [17]

In a great variety of ways the PRC has sought to impress on the people of Taiwan the advantages of incorporation with the mainland: it has stepped up broadcasts from former ROC officials to their friends and relatives in Taiwan; it has invited large numbers of overseas Chinese of Taiwanese origin, especially from Japan and the United States, to visit the mainland; it has granted amnesty to jailed former Nationalist officials and to special service personnel captured in raids on the mainland, providing facilities for their travel to Taiwan if they wish to go there. The PRC no longer attacks members of the Taiwan Independence Movement in the United States and Japan, but invites them to visit the mainland. It has organized on the mainland a Taiwan Democratic Self-Government League, apparently composed of persons of Taiwan origin. It gives special receptions at the Canton fair for "compatriots of Taiwan origin." It has invited Taiwan-born sportsmen to come to China from Japan, the United States, and elsewhere to compete in the national games or to compete for a chance to represent China in the Asian games. It has inaugurated weather broadcasts by the Fukien Front Broadcasting Station of the Peoples' Liberation Army "for the convenience and safety of compatriot fishermen" from Taiwan. The aim of this campaign has been to convince the people of the island that China is making great progress domestically and internationally, that the United States can no longer be relied upon to protect Taiwan, that "liberation" of the island is therefore inevitable, that Taiwan's incorporation into China will not affect adversely the lives of the mass of people there, and that preferred treatment will be given those who contribute to the "liberation."

Taipei's reaction to this campaign has been to reject any suggestion of negotiation with Peking and to reiterate that recovery of the mainland is the ROC's long-term goal. Open expression in Taiwan of views favorable to the PRC is strictly banned, but ROC leaders recognize that there is no practicable way to prevent people from gaining increased access to information on mainland China—both favorable and unfavorable—not only through mainland broadcasts, which have not been very influential, but also through extensive and expanding personal channels. Taipei seeks to counter Peking's influence in part by constant criticism of Chinese communism through the educational system and the public media. But the top officials in Taiwan recognize that in the long run the best means of guarding against the development of sentiment favoring placing Taiwan under PRC control is to demonstrate Taiwan's ability not only to survive, but to continue to widen the gap between the standard of living on the mainland and that on Taiwan under conditions that preserve a substantial measure of personal freedom. Hence, the economic development of the island and the foreign connections on which that depends are all-important.

PRC leaders may be counting on their country's economic development and the growth of its standing and influence in the world, as contrasted with Taiwan's diplomatic isolation, to create a constituency in Taiwan favoring association with the mainland, thereby circumventing a resort to drastic measures to interfere with Taiwan's economic development. Perhaps they anticipate that the severance of diplomatic relations with the United States and an end to the mutual security treaty will in themselves create enough uncertainty concerning Taiwan's future to undermine the stability of the ROC government, shrink its foreign economic relations, and facilitate the creation of a pro-PRC underground on the island. Peking may be willing, as Chou En-lai suggested, to work patiently over a long period of time to bring Taiwan around through a combination of persuasion and mild pressure. Drastic measures may be precluded for some time to come by the uncertainties created by the political struggle in China following Mao's death and the PRC's need to improve relations with the United States and Japan in order to strengthen its position against the U.S.S.R.

Consolidation of a new leadership and a decline of tension with the Soviet Union would make it easier for the PRC to take strong action to squeeze Taiwan's economy. Pressure against Taiwan's trading partners could be aimed at individual firms or at governments. But there are so many firms and so many ways of circumventing PRC attempts to restrict their freedom of action that pressure of this sort would have little effect, as Peking must already have discovered in its effort in 1970 to put pressure on Japanese firms trading with Taiwan. Pressure on governments might be successful in a few instances where the PRC happened to have exceptional leverage on a particular government, but again it is difficult to believe that the PRC would have enough leverage to affect a significant proportion of Taiwan's trade.

Military action is potentially the most effective way of blocking Taiwan's economic relations with the outside world. The PRC could, for example, declare a blockade of Taiwan and use its naval and air power to make it effective. The PRC would be unlikely to take so extreme an action unless it was confident that the United States would not intervene, for it could not make its blockade effective for long against the sea and air power that the United States could bring to bear. If the United States did not intervene, Taiwan's navy and airforce would put up a strong fight, but it seems probable that Peking's much larger airforce and a navy including large numbers of submarines and fast gunboats armed with surface-to-surface missiles would gain control of the sea around Taiwan. PRC losses, especially in the air would be substantial, but presumably tolerable on the assumption that the U.S.S.R. was no longer perceived by Peking as a serious military threat.

Of course, so great a change in Sino-Soviet relations as is assumed in a scenario of this sort would have transformed the East Asian international environment. Use by the PRC of military force to blockade Taiwan, with the U.S.S.R. looking on tolerantly, would further change U.S. perceptions of its interests in the region. The U.S. reaction to such an attack on Taiwan would be subsumed in its larger concern with fortifying its relations with Japan in this new and more threatening environment.

If one adopts the more likely assumption that the PRC would continue to be wary of the U.S.S.R., even though tension between the two nations had somewhat subsided, then a military blockade of Taiwan becomes a more risky operation for the PRC. In that kind of situation would the gain be worth the risks involved in damage to PRC relations with the United States and Japan and the military losses it would suffer in imposing a blockade and perhaps having to follow it up by invasion of Taiwan? Might it not be wiser to wait for the tide of historical inevitability to bring Taiwan into port later, but at less cost?

Taiwan's policy is, of course, designed to make any effort by the PRC to use military force against Taiwan as costly as possible, both politically and militarily, by deepening and widening its relations with the United States and Japan and by strengthening its sea and air power. It has the option of developing nuclear weapons as a deterrent and probably is positioning itself to do so quickly, although the final step is unlikely so long as Taiwan depends heavily on the United

States. Another possible option, should Taiwan's relations with the United States deteriorate badly, is to turn to the U.S.S.R. But the Soviet Union would be unlikely to respond to Taiwan's overtures unless tension with Peking increased and Soviet leaders had given up hope of improving relations with Mao's successors. Still another possible option is for Taiwan to abandon the indefensible offshore islands and declare itself an independent state. Even though few nations might be willing to offend the PRC by according recognition, Taiwan would have weakened Peking's claim to the island in the eyes of the world by this symbolic act. Thus, Taipei's ability to threaten to choose any or all of these three options may inhibit the PRC from attempting crude and direct pressures on Taiwan.

The PRC is not limited, of course, to the use of pressures to achieve its goal of recovering Taiwan; it can also offer inducements. To be effective, however, inducements would have to go far beyond offers to individuals of personal rewards for contributions to "liberation," and vague assurances that incorporation with the mainland would not lower the standard of living on Taiwan. They would have to convince large numbers of people in Taiwan, including a dominant section of the top leadership, that the proposed form of incorporation of Taiwan with the mainland would be more advantageous to them personally than the island's continued existence as a separate political entity.

Personal reasons for fearing the incorporation of Taiwan into the PRC differ, but they create a broad consensus opposing that outcome. Mainlander officials fear not only the loss of their positions, but also the arrest and persecution that befell many of their relatives and associates on the mainland. Businessmen fear the confiscation of their property and a forcible change in their way of life. Politically-minded Taiwanese, who look forward to a larger role in governing

Taiwan as the mainlanders age and die, fear that under the PRC their hopes would be snuffed out by another influx of officials from the mainland. Ordinary citizens fear the imposition over their lives of the kinds of state controls that exist on the mainland and the reduction of their standard of living to the mainland level. Those who have benefited from travel to Japan or the United States fear that the opportunities to travel or study abroad would be severely restricted under a Communist system. The sense of being Chinese and the desire to be a citizen of a historically great and powerful nation exert a persistent impalpable attraction but do not, for most people on Taiwan, offset the personal disadvantages they fear would result from Taiwan's incorporation into the PRC under present circumstances. Thus, it is difficult to conceive of a PRC proposal that would overcome the opposition in Taiwan to the island's incorporation into the PRC.

If the China mainland were a technologically advanced society, it would be better placed to draw Taiwan to itself, but it seems probable that Taiwan's economic development will continue to outpace that of the mainland. Moreover, the tendency to treat with suspicion any proposals by Peking, however generous they might appear, runs deep in Taiwan and is almost certain to persist for a long time. The PRC will probably try to combine pressures and inducements to achieve the maximum effect, but this is a difficult combination to apply effectively. There is a tendency for pressures to cancel out the hoped-for effect of inducement, at least until the capacity and will to resist have been greatly weakened. U.S. policy, and to a lesser extent Japanese policy, toward Taiwan will affect significantly the way the people of Taiwan respond to PRC pressures and inducements.

Over a long period of time new leaders on both sides, less encumbered than their predecessors with fixed ideas, might

[179]

find ways of opening a dialogue. For Peking, such a dialogue would serve as a continuing link between the two parts of China; for Taiwan, it would reduce the danger of military conflict. Ultimately, a framework for peaceful coexistence including trade and travel might be worked out, as it has been between the two Germanies. But no such prospect seems likely in the near future.

U.S. POLICY TOWARD TAIWAN

Since the interests of the United States in Taiwan derive from its broader interest in East Asia, so must policy toward Taiwan conform to the broader policy pattern. Both the relatively short-term question of how to establish formal diplomatic relations with the PRC and the long-term problems of U.S. relations with Taiwan thereafter need to be considered within this broad context.

The Broad Pattern

The United States pursues three objectives in seeking improved relations with the PRC, which transcend the purely bilateral gains from improved relations: (1) to consolidate a stable four-power equilibrium in East Asia and reduce the risk of big-power war; (2) to strengthen the U.S. position in its negotiations with the U.S.S.R.; and (3) to lay the groundwork for eventual PRC cooperation on global problems. Fundamental to the achievement of these objectives is a continued close and cooperative relationship with Japan.

U.S. objectives toward Taiwan are subsidiary to the

[180]

foregoing broader objectives yet closely linked to them. They include reducing the danger of military conflict over Taiwan, and fostering conditions under which the people of Taiwan can continue to maintain a separate political entity unless and until they choose to become associated peacefully with mainland China.

The reaction in the United States to the Shanghai Communiqué demonstrated wide support for the policy of improving relations with the PRC, even at the cost of diminishing relations with Taiwan. Few would quarrel with the view that in the long run the United States must develop closer relations with a nation so large and important as China. But there are significant differences among Americans concerning the urgency of establishing diplomatic relations with the PRC and the price the United States should be willing to pay in cutting back its relations with Taiwan.[18]

Establishment of Diplomatic Relations: The Terms

In the Shanghai Communiqué the United States committed itself in principle to "progress in the normalization of relations between China and the United States" and has from time to time reaffirmed this commitment. "Normalization of relations" has not been defined, but it presumably means upgrading the liaison offices established in 1973 to the status of full-fledged diplomatic missions on conditions acceptable to both sides. The Chinese have stated three conditions for the United States to fulfill: (1) the severance of diplomatic relations with Taipei; (2) the termination of the mutual security treaty with the ROC; and (3) the withdrawal of U.S. military personnel from Taiwan. Thus far the United States has committed itself publicly to only the third condition and has not indicated what,

[181]

if any, reciprocal conditions it might call upon the Chinese to fulfill.

In negotiating the establishment of formal diplomatic relations with Peking, the United States has three options: (1) to accept unconditionally the PRC's three conditions; (2) to accept the PRC's conditions, provided the PRC accepts reciprocal U.S. conditions; or (3) to accept only part of the PRC's conditions.

Unconditional acceptance of the PRC's terms would imply that the United States placed so high a value on improved relations with Peking that U.S. interests in Taiwan could be ignored. Such a position would be difficult to defend within the United States and would risk seriously undermining South Korean and Japanese confidence in the United States. Moreover, given PRC concern over the Soviet threat, the U.S. bargaining position should be strong enough so that it need not accept a completely one-sided agreement. Even the PRC itself would be likely to view such a weak stance as convincing evidence of a further decline in U.S. power and influence in East Asia.

To go to the other extreme, however, and seek to maintain both the security treaty and the present diplomatic relationship with Taipei while establishing diplomatic relations with the PRC is very unlikely to be acceptable to Peking. Much of what the PRC hoped to gain from establishing diplomatic relations with the United States would be cancelled out if Washington continued to maintain formal diplomatic and security relations with Taipei. It is difficult to believe that the post-Mao leadership could afford to accept so much less than it has publicly demanded.

There is, however, a range of possible choices between these two extremes. The easiest to accept, from the U.S. viewpoint, would be the proposal advanced by Senator

Jackson, to recognize the PRC as the government of China and exchange ambassadors with Peking, while replacing the U.S. embassy in Taipei with a "liaison office." Resort to this unconventional form of diplomatic establishment in Taipei would represent a downgrading of U.S. representation there, but would permit the reciprocal granting of diplomatic privileges on a basis similar to that which now prevails between Peking and Washington. Existing treaties and agreements between the Republic of China and the United States could remain in force, although the United States could, if it appeared to be a necessary condition of normalizing relations with the PRC, give the required year's notice that it intended to abrogate the security treaty.

A second possible choice is to establish diplomatic relations with the PRC while ending diplomatic relations with Taiwan, but retaining a consulate there. The presence of U.S. consular officials in Taiwan would greatly facilitate continuing economic and other relations between the two countries, particularly the issuance of visas to residents of Taiwan for travel to the United States. Relatively easy travel to the United States is essential to the maintenance of trade and investment between Taiwan and its largest trading partner and hence is an indispensable condition of Taiwan's economic prosperity. Under U.S. law, which requires the personal appearance of a visa applicant before a consular officer for most types of visas, the United States could not employ the method adopted by Japan of sending visa applications to its consulate in Hong Kong for the issuance of visas. There is a precedent for retaining a consular office in Taiwan. Britain did so from 1950 to 1972 while it had a diplomatic mission in Peking headed by a chargé d'affaires. Although the PRC refused to exchange ambassadors with the United Kingdom so long as the British consulate remained in Taiwan, it would not necessarily take the same position with the United States, since normalization of relations with the United States is more important to the PRC than it was with the UK. In agreeing to the exchange of liaison offices, the PRC has already demonstrated the unique importance it attaches to relations with the United States. Termination of diplomatic relations with the Republic of China would presumably render invalid the government-to-government agreements it has with the United States, including the security treaty. Substitutes for the most important of these would have to be devised if serious deterioration of Taiwan's security and economy were to be prevented.

A third choice differs from the above only in replacing the U.S. embassy in Taiwan with a non-official organization staffed by professional diplomats on temporary detail, rather than a consulate. This choice would resemble the "Japanese model," which PRC officials have indicated they would accept. Like the second choice, it would require substitutes for existing government-to-government agreements and would present more difficult technical and legal problems for the United States than the retention of a consulate, for there are few precedents in international law for this type of arrangement.

The most important objectives for both Washington and Peking in normalizing relations are to gain leverage relative to the U.S.S.R. and to avoid the high tension and dangerous military confrontations that characterized their relations during the 1950s and 1960s. Their ability to move forward in this area of common interest is hampered by sharp divergence of their interests regarding Taiwan. The United States would like to normalize on terms that accorded the people of Taiwan the largest feasible degree of freedom to decide their own future. The PRC would prefer the terms that most weakened Taiwan's capability to resist future PRC pressures and inducements. Thus, the United States would prefer the first choice above, preferably without ending the security treaty, while the PRC would prefer the third choice. What terms to accept requires difficult judgments on both sides as to how much they value the improved international position represented by normalization over the costs that would be incurred—by the United States in weakening its connections with Taiwan, and by the PRC in acquiescing in a continuing U.S. relationship with Taiwan. Both will also have to decide whether the costs of failing to reach agreement on normalization would outweigh the costs of accepting a less than satisfactory arrangement on Taiwan.

The actions that the PRC asks of the United States are more difficult in a way than those which the United States might ask of the PRC, for they require concrete actions, such as breaking diplomatic relations with the Republic of China or ending the security treaty which, once taken, would not be easy to reverse. The United States has never broken diplomatic relations with a friendly government or abrogated a security treaty. The ending of the security treaty would have repercussions adverse to U.S. interests not only in Taiwan, but among other U.S. allies, especially those in East Asia, and would encounter domestic opposition. The much less explicit PRC assurances, on the other hand, concerning its tolerance of U.S.-Taiwan relations and the expected improvements in U.S.-PRC relations would be easier to back away from. It would be impossible for the United States to restore the status quo ante should the PRC decide a few years after normalization that a lessening of tension with the U.S.S.R. enabled it to renege on its assurances to the United States and to adopt a hard line on Taiwan. Of course, in that event, the United States would have the option of encouraging the government on Taiwan to declare its formal independence and recognizing it as a state. The existence of this option should be a strong deterrent to any blatant violation of its assurances by the PRC.

It is difficult for an outsider to judge in advance what terms the PRC might accept in negotiations on normalization. That could be determined definitely only in the course of the negotiations themselves. But it seems probable that the PRC would insist that the United States end the security treaty and terminate formal diplomatic relations with Taiwan. Whether the PRC could be persuaded to acquiesce in a U.S. liaison office or consulate in Taiwan is uncertain. Such an arrangement would go beyond the "Japanese model," which PRC officials have indicated they could accept, but the United States is, after all, not Japan and should be in a position to insist on different treatment. The replacement of the U.S. embassy in Taiwan by a liaison office and the ending of the security treaty would constitute a substantial weakening of U.S.-Taiwan relations which might well be acceptable to Peking if the alternative were the continuation of the present U.S. relationships with Taiwan and the PRC.

In any arrangement that required ending the security treaty, the key questions for the United States are how far the Chinese would be willing to go in committing themselves to the peaceful resolution of the Taiwan problem, and whether their assurances would satisfy the U.S. administration's need to answer domestic and foreign criticisms that the United States had abandoned an ally to military conquest. The Chinese have long insisted, in the Warsaw talks (held intermittently with the United States—initially in Geneva—between 1953 and 1970) and elsewhere, that they could never renounce the right to use force against Taiwan if necessary. To do otherwise would undercut their claims to sovereignty over Taiwan. Consequently, the United States would probably have to accept something less than a clearcut renunciation of force. In any case, the main guarantee of Taiwan's security would not be PRC assurances, but the military and political costs to Peking of using force against Taiwan.

Various formulae could be devised to meet the need for an understanding between Washington and Peking that the probability of the use of force against Taiwan would be low. For example, Peking would retain the right to use force, while disclaiming any intention to use it. The United States would permit the treaty to lapse, but make clear its strong opposition to any attempt to settle the Taiwan question by force. Peking would be aware that the United States retained the capability to intervene even without security treaty, should it decide its interests required it.

Taiwan's security also requires continued access to military equipment from the United States. Whether the United States should make the right to supply military equipment an explicit condition for normalization of relations is a difficult question of tactics. One could argue that the United States should establish a clear position on this issue in the bargaining process leading up to the establishment of diplomatic relations in order to avoid future misunderstanding and trouble. But this would be a difficult condition for the PRC to accept explicitly. The United States probably would be better advised, therefore, to take an explicit position on this issue only if the PRC raises it. The U.S. intention to continue to sell weapons to the ROC could be made clear outside the negotiating forum in such a way that the PRC would not be compelled to react. Moreover, U.S. intentions would be implicit in the strong U.S. opposition to the use of force to settle the Taiwan issue and in the continuance of a wide range of economic and other relations between the United States and Taiwan. The United States should, however, be prepared to end military credit sales to Taiwan and should encourage the government of the ROC to purchase weapons from Europe as well as the United States.

Like Japan, Canada, the United Kingdom and many other countries, the United States should avoid taking the position that Taiwan is legally a part of the People's Republic of China. Moreover, if the United States totally severs diplomatic relations with the Republic of China, retaining only a consular office or non-official representation in Taiwan, and all existing government-to-government agreements terminate, [19] it should be prepared to take immediate legislative and administrative action to provide a new legal basis for the provision of military equipment and to ensure uninterrupted economic relations between the United States and Taiwan. Failure to act promptly to provide substitutes for these agreements would create grave risk of panic in Taiwan. These include such essential agreements as the basic treaty of commerce, friendship, and navigation and agreements on the civil uses of atomic energy, civil air transport, investment guarantees, the loan of destroyers and other naval ships, and quotas on textile shipments to the United States. Indispensable to Taiwan's economic survival is most-favored-nation treatment for its imports, as extended at present by the treaty of commerce; otherwise, Taiwan's products would be excluded by ruinously high tariffs.

Establishment of Diplomatic Relations: The Timing

Until 1976 the case could be made that the United States should move promptly to establish diplomatic relations with the PRC while Mao Tse-tung and Chou En-lai were still living. It was argued that they had indicated willingness to tolerate extensive continuing relations between the United States and Taiwan, whereas no one could predict the position their successors might take. Moreover, Mao was known to be adamantly anti-Soviet, while his successor might be disposed to improve relations with the U.S.S.R.

With the death of Mao and Chou, the argument for moving quickly to establish formal diplomatic relations with the PRC is much weakened. Indeed, it would be prudent to defer initiating negotiations with the PRC on this subject until Hua Kuo-feng has consolidated his position as Mao's successor. A leader who was not firmly in control and lacked confidence in his own position probably would not be able to agree to the safeguards which the United States would insist on for its future relations with Taiwan. The failure of a premature attempt to reach agreement with Hua would adversely affect U.S. relations with the PRC and would result in delaying rather than expediting the establishment of diplomatic relations.

The beginning of negotiations should not be deferred indefinitely, however. It is desirable to strengthen the under-standing reached in the Shanghai Communiqué that the Taiwan issue should not stand in the way of the improvement of relations between Washington and Peking and to underline the U.S. position that the ultimate resolution of the Taiwan issue should be peaceful. In order to reinforce this framework on which the improvement of Washington-Peking relations has been based, the United States must take further steps toward completing the process of "normalization" to which it is pledged; failure to move ahead probably would lead to regression, for the present status is inherently unstable. Assuming that Hua does succeed in consolidating his position as the new leader of China, the United States could begin sounding out senior Chinese officials on the question of Taiwan to determine whether conditions were favorable for undertaking formal negotiations. The United States will be in

[189]

a strong bargaining position so long as tension between Moscow and Peking is high. It would be well to consolidate the basis for improved relations with the PRC under relatively favorable conditions, rather than take the risk that prolonged inaction could be exploited by those within China who favor improving relations with the Soviet Union rather than with the United States.

The Long-term Outlook

The Taiwan issue obviously will not be resolved by the establishment of formal diplomatic relations between the United States and the PRC. It will, however, have entered a new stage, in which the United States and the PRC will continue to have strong reasons for wanting to keep their differences over Taiwan from interfering with the promotion of more important interests.

The broad U.S. objectives in East Asia cited above do not demand any particular ultimate solution of the Taiwan issue. Provided the solution is peacefully arrived at, the United States could accept either an independent Taiwan, acquiesced to by the PRC, or the integration of Taiwan into the PRC, or, falling between these extremes, a loose association of Taiwan with the PRC. But none of these solutions is likely to be arrived at soon. For a long time the United States will have to cope with an ambiguous situation. Its policy could tilt toward independence or integration—or it could seek to minimize its influence in either direction.

A tilt toward the ultimate emergence of Taiwan as an independent state would be in line with the most probable trends in Taiwan itself. But U.S. encouragement of Taiwan to move in this direction would be seen in Peking and elsewhere as contravening the position taken by the United States in the Shanghai Communiqué and would become a serious obstacle to improving relations with the PRC. On the other hand, a tilt which would put pressure on Taiwan to integrate with the PRC, while beneficial initially to U.S. relations with the PRC, would be likely to create turmoil in Taiwan and acts of desperation on the part of its leaders that could then force very distasteful choices on the United States. It would have a divisive effect domestically in the United States and would risk serious damage to U.S. relations with South Korea and Japan. It might result ultimately in damaging U.S.-PRC relations also. Moreover, a U.S. policy that takes into account the wishes and welfare of the people of Taiwan would be likely to receive greater support among the American people than a policy of writing them off.

The course of action for the United States least likely to interfere with the achievement of its broader objectives in the region would be to loosen its connections with Taiwan gradually without prejudging Taiwan's ultimate status. It would serve the interests of the United States, the PRC, and the people of Taiwan also that the island become less dependent on the United States, provided the change took place gradually over a period of years, avoiding sudden, severe shocks to the political system in Taiwan. Such a policy would create the best atmosphere for an ultimate peaceful solution of the problem and in the meantime would make it easier for all parties to live with.

The United States would seek to convince the PRC, on the one hand, that a military attack on Taiwan would involve grave risks, but, on the other hand, that the United States would not oppose peaceful reintegration of Taiwan with the mainland. The United States would also have to convince the PRC that it was not conniving to create an independent state

[191]

of Taiwan or to enable Taiwan to acquire nuclear weapons—and that a substantial degree of continuing U.S. involvement with Taiwan was necessary to prevent either of these contingencies.

At the same time, the United States would seek to convince the leaders in Taiwan that their interests would be best served by not declaring independence or going nuclear. Either action would be seen by Peking as a provocation and would inflame the issue with unpredictable consequences. The interests of all parties would be better served by keeping Taiwan's status ambiguous and its visibility low.

The PRC would find Taiwan's *de facto* separate status easier to tolerate if some kind of communication and interaction were to develop between Taiwan and the mainland. For the time being, there is little the United States could or should do to encourage this. The government in Taiwan fears that any contact would facilitate Peking's efforts to subvert the people of Taiwan. After it has gained confidence, however, that Taiwan can continue to survive and prosper even without formal diplomatic relations with the United States, it may see advantages in some controlled intercourse. Informal intercommunication seems certain to increase in any case because of the multiplying relations that both Taiwan and the PRC will have with other parts of the world, especially Hong Kong and Japan.

The critical variable in the Taiwan issue between the United States and the PRC is the state of Sino-Soviet relations, which is determined by factors far removed from Taiwan. So long as Sino-Soviet tension remains high, it will be difficult for the PRC to take actions on the Taiwan issue that would damage its relations with the United States and Japan. This situation affords substantial scope for the United States and Japan to maintain their informal relations with Taiwan. If

Sino-Soviet relations should improve so greatly as to give Peking a much freer hand in bringing pressure to bear on Taiwan, the United States and Japan would have to review their policies toward Taiwan in the light of the changed conditions.

NOTES

1. A senior Japanese diplomat told me in March 1972 that he expected the United States to be well advanced in negotiating full diplomatic relations with Peking by the end of that year, that Taiwan would collapse politically within five years, and that he was advising Japanese businessmen to withdraw their capital from Taiwan. This extreme view was not widely shared within the Japanese Foreign Ministry; but officials there, still reeling from the "Nixon shock" of July 1971, were very uncertain of American intentions toward Taiwan.

2. *Department of State Bulletin,* January 16, 1950, p. 79.

3. *Department of State Bulletin,* July 3, 1950, p. 5.

4. *New York Times,* January 25, 1976, August 30, 1976; U.S. Embassy, Taipei.

5. Asked whether the United States should withdraw diplomatic recognition from Nationalist China in order to establish relations with the PRC, 70 percent of those questioned were opposed, while only 10 percent favored such a move. *A Gallup Study of Public Attitudes Toward Nations of the World,* Conducted for the Chinese Information Service, Republic of China, October 1975, p. 17.

6. International Monetary Fund/IBRD, *Direction of Trade,* September 1976, pp. 36, 37.

7. *Japan Times Weekly* (International Edition), March 27, 1976, p. 3.

8. As compared to 256,000 in 1971, the year before the severance of diplomatic relations. Japanese visitors far outnumber the second most numerous foreign visitors, the Americans, who numbered 117,000 in 1974. Economic Planning Council, Republic of China, *Taiwan Statistical Data Book,* 1975, p. 113.

9. *Asahi,* October 1, 1972.

10. A leading Japanese expert on China told me he estimates that about 100 or more than one-third of the LDP members of the House of Representatives are to some extent "pro-Taiwan"; 80 of them went to Taiwan to attend Chiang Kai-shek's funeral in April 1975.

11. The ratio of the difference in incomes between the top 20 percent of income recipients compared to the bottom 20 percent fell from 15 to 1 in the early 1950s to 5 to 1 by the late 1960s (at a time when the disparity was increasing to 16 to 1 in Mexico and 25 to 1 in Brazil.) James P. Grant, *Growth from Below: A People-Oriented Development Strategy* (Washington, D.C.: Overseas Development Council, December 1973), p. 23.

12. The average annual net capital inflow between 1969 and 1973 was only $42.8 million, a relatively insignificant contribution to gross domestic capital formation, which rose from $1.2 billion to $1.8 billion during this five-year period. On the other hand, the $883 million net capital inflow in 1974 helped to cover an exceptionally large deficit in payments for goods and services of $1.1 billion. *Taiwan Statistical Data Book,* 1975, pp. 40 and 168.

13. International Institute for Strategic Studies, *The Military Balance, 1975-76* (London, 1976), pp. 53-54.

14. U.S. Arms Control and Disarmament Agency, *World Military Expenditures and Arms Transfers, 1965-74,* pp. 24, 27, and 33.

15. Foreign Broadcast Information Service, *Daily Report, East Asia and Pacific,* September 24, 1975, p. B1.

16. International Institute for Strategic Studies, *The Military Balance, 1974-75* (London, 1975), pp. 49-50, 53-54.

17. Jo Yung-hwan, ed., *Taiwan's Future* (Hong Kong: Union Research Institute, for Arizona State University, 1974), pp. 65-70.

18. See note 5, above, and the resolution sponsored by Representative Dawson Mathis in early 1976 (not put to vote), signed by 218 members of the House of Representatives, which called on the U.S. government "while engaged in the lessening of tension with the People's Republic of China, to do nothing to compromise the freedom of our friend and ally, the Republic of China." Senator Henry M. Jackson, on his return from a trip to the PRC in 1974 declared that "we should try to reverse the location of our Embassy and liaison office as between Taipei and Peking." Thomas L. Hughes, former Director of the State Department's Bureau of Intelligence and Research, sharply criticized the administration for not establishing diplomatic relations with Peking on President Ford's trip to China in November 1975. "The China Bungle," *New Republic,* Feb. 28, 1976, pp. 17-23. Varying views were expressed by witnesses before the Subcommittee on Investigations and the Subcommittee on Future Foreign Policy of the House International Relations Committee at hearings held in January and March 1976.

19. See U.S. Department of State, *Treaties in Force: A List of Treaties and Other International Agreements of the United States in Force on January 1, 1975,* pp. 51-56, for a list of existing agreements.

SIX

China in
American Foreign Policy

William J. Barnds

The attempt of the Nixon Administration to establish a new relationship with Peking launched the United States upon an uncharted course in its China policy. Historically, America either had dealt with a weak but relatively friendly China, or had contended with a relatively strong but hostile China. (In reality, Chinese friendship before the Communists rose to power was never as strong as most Americans believed, nor was China as powerful or as dangerous in the 1950s and 1960s as Americans thought at the time.) Now the United States— itself confused and divided over its proper role in the world— was trying anew to forge a constructive relationship with Asia's largest nation.

The opening to China reversed, at least for a time, America's eroding position and prestige around the world. It demonstrated that the United States, despite the trauma of Vietnam, was capable of recognizing and dealing decisively with the realities of power in a new and more complex international environment. It also meant that the Soviet Union could no longer avoid the full impact its conflict with China was having on its position in the world. The Sino-Soviet split had undermined Moscow's authority over the world Communist movement and spurred polycentrism during the 1960s, but China's withdrawal into isolation during the Cultural Revolution and America's deepening involvement in Vietnam had enabled the Soviet Union to avoid many of the potential costs of its quarrel with Peking in the arena of world politics. The thaw in Sino-American relations gave the United States the opportunity to take advantage of Sino-Soviet hostility through its triangular diplomacy, a possibility that had been analyzed with great insight by Michel Tatu.[1]

As the Soviets could not openly object to an improvement in Sino-American relations, they were cautious in their reactions. Yet they were obviously worried that both the United States and China would be in stronger positions to deal with the U.S.S.R.[2] Moscow could take consolation from the strain that the overture to Peking created in Japanese-American relations, but could not bring itself to deal flexibly enough with Tokyo to take advantage of the opportunity. The similarity between the Chinese and American positions during India's military intervention in Bangladesh in late 1971 was cited by Soviet commentators as an example of the type of Sino-American collusion that could strengthen their cooperation as well as their individual interests at Soviet expense, and perhaps even endanger the Soviet-American détente.

Perhaps the most remarkable aspect of the new policy—made more dramatic by Henry Kissinger's secret visit to Peking in 1971 and by President Nixon's triumphal visit in February 1972—was its widespread popularity among the American people. For two decades, bitterness and hostility had

[197]

dominated American attitudes toward Peking. Now a staunchly anti-Communist President won the acclaim of most Americans and the acquiescence of nearly all the rest in his efforts to arrange a détente with the nation that Americans had long regarded as their most implacable—if not their most dangerous—adversary.

The dramatic nature of the opening to China, combined with the resurgence of American fascination with China and the Chinese flair for hospitality, led many Americans to conclude that a new era of Sino-American friendship and cooperation had been inaugurated. Inflated expectations of the kind of relationship that was possible quickly arose, and these hopes were encouraged by the substantial progress made between 1971 and late 1973 in strengthening relations. But since late 1973 there has been little if any forward movement. The combination of President Nixon's need for conservative support during the Watergate upheaval and the Communist victory in Vietnam led the United States to maintain its diplomatic and treaty ties with the Republic of China. The failure to shift recognition from Taipei to Peking, the perception of some Chinese leaders of a weakening American resolve to counter Soviet expansionism, the illnesses and deaths of Chou En-lai and Mao Tse-tung, and the American election campaign together led to a stalemate in relations.

Thus significant obstacles—especially the thorny problem of U.S. relations with the Republic of China (Taiwan)—remain to be overcome before the normalization of Sino-American relations set forth as a goal in the Shanghai Communiqué can be achieved. Beyond that, basic questions involving the kind of relationship that is feasible between two such different societies remain to be answered. There is an awareness among Americans of the need for a measure of Sino-American cooperation. Trade and cultural exchanges are the major

[198]

elements of the bilateral aspect of the relationship, but neither government regards these as the key elements in their policies. Official statements that Sino-American ties are not directed against third parties do not obscure the fact that both Chinese and Americans, despite their differences on many important international issues, want to use the other to check the Soviet Union. Do the differences between the two societies, and the contrasts between their world views, mean that the elements of cooperation will remain clearly subordinate to those of competition in the relationship, and that serious conflicts over specific issues are inevitable from time to time? If so, such an ambivalent relationship will pose difficult problems for any administration, given the inclination of the American people to regard other countries either as friends or enemies. Or are there possibilities of political cooperation that would gradually shift the character of the relationship? Answers to such questions can only be formulated in the broader context of American foreign policy toward Asia and, to a degree, the world at large. Moreover, they will depend upon Chinese as well as American moves, and will be affected by the legacy of the past three decades, which the efforts of the past few years have not yet overcome.

America's China Policy: 1944-77

United States policy toward China over the last thirty years falls fairly neatly into three periods. The first of these, from shortly before the end of World War II until 1950, was largely a time of attempting to adjust to unforeseen and unpalatable developments. The second, from the outbreak of the Korean War until the early 1970s, was a period of bitter hostility—although U.S. attitudes and policies shifted from

[199]

time to time within the framework of a basic antagonism. The third period, since the early 1970s, has featured a search for a new but still ill-defined relationship.

From Friendship to Animosity.

During the early years of the war against the Japanese the American people displayed one of their characteristic weaknesses in foreign policy, namely, a tendency to idolize their allies while regarding their enemies as the personification of evil. President Roosevelt insisted that China be treated as one of the major powers and be given a permanent seat in the Security Council of the United Nations. Such a decision probably stemmed from a conviction that a strong and stable China was necessary if Japanese militarism was to be held in check over the long run, as well as from an assumption that a strong China would continue to cooperate with the United States.[3] As the war went on, President Roosevelt found Chiang Kai-shek a stubborn and difficult partner and the Chinese Nationalists' war effort an increasing disappointment. The concessions the United States made to Stalin at China's expense to induce the U.S.S.R. to enter the war against Japan suggest that Roosevelt's confidence in China's ability to play a key role had declined over the years.

The accelerating erosion of the Nationalist position and the growing power of the Communists after 1944 created a basic dilemma for the U.S. government as it sought to keep China either from civil war and chaos or from being controlled by a Communist government, which many thought would represent an extension of Soviet power. America's difficulties were increased by the fact that most of the government's attention, energy, and resources in the early postwar years had to be

[200]

directed toward meeting the Soviet challenge in Central Europe and the Eastern Mediterranean. United States leaders were also handicapped by inadequate knowledge and conflicting reports about developments in China. Presidents Roosevelt and Truman and their advisers had three broad choices open to them.[4] They could take whatever steps were necessary, including direct U.S. military involvement, to prevent a Communist victory. They could try to bring about an arrangement for sharing power between the Nationalists and the Communists. Or the United States could withdraw completely from the Chinese political arena once the Japanese forces had been disarmed and repatriated.

The first option appeared far too costly and uncertain, especially as Nationalist weaknesses became ever more apparent and serious. Moreover, although American power remained impressive, rapid demobilization was the order of the day, thus foreclosing military intervention. The United States nevertheless favored the Nationalists, especially by transporting their forces to northern and eastern China to accept the surrender of Japanese forces, but was determined not to involve its own forces in any fighting between rival Chinese groups.

The third choice, a policy of completely jettisoning the Nationalists, also appeared to have serious drawbacks. The Chinese Nationalists were America's allies, and had strong and active—if gradually declining—support in Congress and among the American people. The Cold War was beginning. The attitude of the Chinese Communists toward Moscow was uncertain, but it seemed likely to most U.S. officials that they would, at a minimum, lean toward the Soviet Union. Nonetheless, the Communists had impressed some American officials and observers in China with their dedication and efficiency, and these Americans argued that the Communists were not only concerned with the welfare of the Chinese people but also independent of the Soviet Union. Moreover, as long as the Communists had some hope that the United States would force Chiang Kai-shek to share power with them, they naturally withheld criticism of the United States and tried to convince U.S. officials that they could and would work with America.

Thus the decision was made to send General Marshall to try to bring the contending forces together, while at the same time continuing to provide economic assistance and arms to the Nationalists. The attempt to induce two such bitter antagonists to share power was unrealistic, but such knowledge as American leaders had of Chinese affairs and political culture was limited, and the unpalatability of the alternative courses led them to this policy. When attempts to bring the two sides together failed by early 1947, the United States continued a policy of half-hearted support for the Nationalists.

Such policies antagonized the Communists while failing to sustain the Nationalists. Continued U.S. support of the Nationalists was one factor which shifted the perspectives and policy of the Communists between 1945 and 1947, and they began to attack the United States with mounting vehemence. Moreover, by 1947 the Cold War with the Soviet Union had begun in earnest, and it would have been extremely difficult politically for the Chinese Communists to have defied Stalin—then at the height of his prestige—and cooperated in any meaningful fashion with the United States under such conditions. (Extremely difficult, but not impossible. By 1948 Tito showed that a Communist leader, if pressed hard enough, might break with Moscow; and, by providing assistance to Yugoslavia, the United States demonstrated that balance-of-power considerations could override anti-communism in certain circumstances.)

[202]

Even in 1949, when the Communists won control of the mainland and the remnants of Chiang's forces fled to Taiwan, Peking and Washington might have worked out a formally correct relationship rather than an actively hostile one. Huang Hua, a leading Communist official, approached Ambassador Leighton Stewart in April 1949, indicating an interest in U.S. recognition. The United States responded to this Chinese Communist probe by indicating that it was willing to consider diplomatic recognition under appropriate circumstances, but not until the new government was established, which did not occur until October 1949. On June 30, 1949, Mao proclaimed that China would "lean to one side" because "internationally, we belong to the side of the anti-imperialist front headed by the Soviet Union, and so can turn only to this side for genuine and friendly help, not to the side of the imperialist front . . ."[5] The Communist leaders thus let their outlook and actions be guided more by the fact that the United States had provided *limited* aid to Chiang Kai-shek than that it had refused to give him *full* support. They arrested, mistreated, and deported U.S. officials and seized American property, which hardened U.S. attitudes. Chinese support, even if largely verbal, for Communist revolts against newly independent Asian countries also clearly worried U.S. officials.

The Truman Administration's attempts to deal with rising public attacks on its China policy had little success, and were flawed by a basic misconception if not an outright contradiction. Secretary of State Acheson's August 5, 1949, letter of transmittal of the China White Paper attributed the Nationalists' defeat to their own shortcomings, which, he argued, were beyond America's power to remedy or offset. At the same time that Acheson emphasized the domestic Chinese causes of the Communist victory, he maintained that Mao's statement that China would "lean to one side" and ally itself with the

[203]

Soviet Union meant that the Chinese leaders were making their country subservient to Moscow.

In January 1950 President Truman announced that the United States would not defend Taiwan, and in the same month Acheson excluded the island from America's *primary* defense perimeter in Asia. Despite the signing of the Sino-Soviet treaty in February 1950, the U.S. government remained willing to accept Communist control of the island. However, the United States still held back from withdrawing diplomatic recognition from the Republic of China and opposed granting Peking the Chinese seat in the United Nations. The crescendo of Republican attacks on the Administration's China policy, the Chinese Communists' harsh treatment of Americans, and popular American feelings of frustration and anger at the trend of events in China all combined to delay any decisive move on the question of recognition until the possibility was overtaken by events.

Two Decades of Hostility

North Korea's invasion of South Korea in June 1950 set in motion a chain of events that made China and the United States enemies for two decades. The American decision to protect Taiwan with the Seventh Fleet while coming to the assistance of a beleaguered South Korea re-injected the United States into the Chinese civil war. The smashing Chinese offensive against the U.S. forces following the destruction of the North Korean army and the reckless march of the victorious American forces toward the Yalu River stunned and infuriated American opinion. The U.S. government had not expected the Communists to resort to open war, but they had done so in Korea. Many Americans, remembering China's century of disarray, had expected the Chinese Communists to have great difficulty controlling and organizing their vast country—if indeed they were able to do so at all. Now they had demonstrated that they could not only organize the country but defeat American armies on the battlefield as well. United States public opinion hardened, and critics who questioned America's hard-line China policy were intimidated and then silenced. (The fact that this image of Communist strength was accompanied by a belief in many American minds that the Chinese people would overthrow such an "alien" regime was but another of the contradictions that bedeviled U.S. efforts to develop a coherent policy.)

As a result of these developments, coming within a few years of the communization of Eastern Europe, there arose in American minds the image of a worldwide Communist movement of incredible unity and dynamism. Only the United States stood between the Communists and something approaching world domination, and there was a pervasive feeling in American minds that if the United States and the West suffered any further losses to the Communists the free world position would become untenable. This feeling that further losses were intolerable created a climate of fear in American thinking, which in turn contributed to a rigidity in both outlook and policy. These attitudes were skillfully exploited by the "China Lobby" and in the 1950s led to a purge of many China specialists in government accused of being pro-Communist or even of not being sufficiently strong in their backing of the Nationalists. Later the Committee of One Million Against the Admission of Communist China to the United Nations limited any American flexibility.[6]

The Communist victory in the Chinese civil war and Peking's entry into the Korean war also led to the extension of the containment policy from Europe to Asia. Aid to the

French fighting against the Vietminh in Indochina began in 1950. Japan became the cornerstone of the U.S. position in East Asia. An arrangement was worked out to end the Occupation and sign a peace treaty, but only on the condition that Tokyo sign a peace treaty with Taipei rather than Peking, and that it also sign a security treaty giving the United States continuing base rights in Japan. Moreover, the United States insisted on retaining full control of Okinawa, although it recognized Japan's "residual sovereignty." The United States obtained most of what it wanted from Japan, but Tokyo refused to bend to strong U.S. pressures that it re-arm.

The effort to contain and isolate China was intensified and institutionalized after the election of Dwight Eisenhower to the presidency and the appointment of John Foster Dulles as Secretary of State. The United States signed mutual security treaties with various Asian nations, partly in order to carry out its evolving strategic design, but also partly in an effort to deal with local problems as they arose.[7] Defense treaties were signed with South Korea in 1953 and the Republic of China in 1954, and the Southeast Asia Treaty Organization (SEATO) was also established in 1954. If the Chinese were hostile, and the Communist world was willing to resort to aggression to achieve its aims, American leaders felt they had little alternative to strengthening any non-Communist forces around the periphery of China that would cooperate with the West. Even the offshore islands lying but a few miles from the China coast were deemed to be worth the involvement of American prestige and resources lest their fall undermine the morale of the Chinese Nationalists on Taiwan. (The United States did persuade Taipei to evacuate the Tachens, the least important and least defensible of the offshore islands, but the key islands of Quemoy and Matsu were reinforced—a symbol to both Nationalists and Communists that there was but one China.)

Three points about U.S. policy toward Asia in general and China in particular during the Eisenhower-Dulles years should be noted. *First,* the security system created by the United States to contain China was constructed piecemeal and was unintegrated. Japan and South Korea did not even establish diplomatic relations until 1965. While on paper SEATO was a multilateral treaty, what strength it had was largely supplied by U.S. backing for its individual Asian members—and indirectly by British support of Malaya and Singapore outside the treaty. Important countries, such as India and Indonesia, were actively opposed to the whole U.S. undertaking. Even so, the idea that the Cold War, which was stalemated in Europe and East Asia by the mid-1950s, could be won or lost in the Third World led some important U.S. officials to argue for large-scale American economic aid to India on the ground that India and China were contending for the leadership of Asia, and whichever was the more successful in furthering economic development would become the leader of the continent. While such ideas were put forward most vigorously by American liberals, they had other supporters as well. In 1953 Secretary Dulles stated that

There is occurring between the two countries (India and China) a competition as to whether ways of freedom or police state methods can achieve better social progress. This competition affects directly 800 million people in these two countries. In the long run, the outcome will affect all of humanity, including ourselves.[8]

Other Americans advocated fostering Indo-Japanese cooperation to contain China, a scheme which overlooked the contrasting outlooks and policies of the two countries as well as their disinterest in each other and their inability to work closely together.

Second, in contrast to the situation in Western Europe, the United States had no major power (such as Britain or France) as an ally. Japan's recent status as an enemy nation, combined with its military weakness and opposition to involvement in power politics, eliminated the possibility of its playing any such role. Thus the United States missed the benefits that derive from working out a policy in consultation with an ally that is friendly but strong enough so that its views have to be weighed carefully. A special feeling of American responsibility combined with the bitterness about the Chinese rejection of our friendship were hardly the ingredients for a successful policy. (Henry Kissinger, before he entered government, once commented that Americans regarded the United States as having "responsibilities" whereas other countries had "interests.")

Third, there was little indication that U.S. policy was based upon the goal of being able to negotiate from strength with China, as it was with the Soviet Union. Continued recognition of the Republic of China, concerns about the weakness of the non-Communist Asian governments, widespread popular antagonism toward the Chinese Communists, and a combination of hope and belief that the Communist regime in Peking was a passing phenomenon all worked to give American policy an essentially negative cast.[9] Thus when Chou En-lai offered at Bandung in 1955 to negotiate with the United States about relaxing tensions in the Far East, the United States responded only by agreeing to raise the consular talks begun a year earlier in Geneva to the ambassadorial level, but the talks made progress only on facilitating the repatriation of civilians who desired to return to their respective countries. American leaders were not only trapped by domestic public opinion, but

[208]

also feared that the entire structure of alliances they were attempting to construct might collapse if they responded more favorably to what many regarded as no more than a Chinese attempt to create complacency and confusion.[10]

In fairness to American officials, it should be emphasized that the pattern of events in China from the mid-1950s on was an erratic one. The outpouring of criticism that took place during the Hundred Flowers Campaign demonstrated that there *was* considerable opposition to important policies of the government, and perhaps to the regime itself. Chinese policy hardened considerably in the late 1950s, and reckless Chinese rhetoric obscured Peking's greater caution in action. The impressive energy and dramatic claims associated with the Great Leap Forward were quickly followed by the admission of serious errors and setbacks, and famine in the early 1960s was only averted by large-scale food imports. The development of the Sino-Soviet dispute at a time China still felt threatened by the United States had not been foreseen and appeared to indicate Chinese recklessness, as did Mao's apparently casual acceptance of the idea of nuclear war. Finally, the shift in Sino-Indian relations from at least superficial friendship to open hostility was puzzling, and Peking's actions in the 1962 Sino-Indian war (which were widely misinterpreted) revived Western fears of Chinese aggressiveness and expansionism.

China's erratic course and bitter hostility were both puzzling and disappointing to President Kennedy, who had been critical of the rigidity of past American policy toward China. He had favored the evacuation of the offshore islands, though not under the threat of Chinese attack. The Kennedy Administration had no illusions about the durability of the Communist regime. But the willingness of Kennedy and some of his advisers to explore, if only hesitantly, some type of a

[209]

two-China solution made him seem doubly dangerous to Mao and his colleagues. Mao's personal denunciation of the President and attack on the nuclear test-ban treaty, which Kennedy regarded as one of his major achievements, convinced him that he was caught between a rigid foe in Peking and an inflexible public opinion at home, and that there were few changes he could make in America's China policy.

But if no significant changes in policy were feasible, there was the beginning of a change in atmosphere in the United States regarding China, starting around 1960. Despite China's erratic course and stridently voiced hostility toward the United States, American scholars specializing on China increasingly stressed several points. The strains in Sino-Soviet relations first made it apparent not only that China was no Soviet satellite or puppet, but that Peking and Moscow were becoming steadily more hostile to one another. If China was reckless in word it was proving cautious in deed; Chinese military moves in Korea in 1950 and against India in 1962 were, it began to be argued, defensive rather than aggressive or expansionist—at least in Peking's eyes.[11] Moreover, the explosion of China's first nuclear device in October 1964 heightened the need to think in terms of some sort of accommodation with China.

None of these views had any immediate or dramatic influence on U.S. policy. Indeed, Sino-American relations deteriorated with the growing U.S. involvement in Vietnam but, as with China's nuclear explosion, made both sides aware of the costs and dangers of continuing confrontation. The bombing of North Vietnam was a particular concern of the Chinese leaders, and policy debate about the appropriate Chinese response became caught up in internal politics. However, U.S. leaders made clear that they had no intention of attacking China, and the Chinese leaders concluded that the

Vietnamese struggle must be carried out by the Vietnamese themselves, although China would supply them with aid. American expressions of hope for better relations were indignantly rejected by the Chinese, who were already smarting under Soviet accusations that Peking's aid to Vietnam was more verbal than material. Moreover, China was entering the Cultural Revolution, an upheaval that virtually suspended serious Chinese foreign policy moves for three years.

Forging a New Relationship.

Two events in the late 1960s made it both necessary and possible for China and the United States to undertake basic foreign policy reappraisals, which in turn led them to search for ways to establish a less hostile relationship. The first was the stalemate in Vietnam, and specifically the Tet Offensive, which made it clear to the American government and public that success in Vietnam—at least as previously defined—was impossible at an acceptable cost. Since the struggle in Vietnam had been presented by U.S. leaders as the logical extension of the general policy of containing communism, the whole policy came into question.

The second change was the growing Chinese fear of the U.S.S.R., as a result of the 1968 Soviet invasion of Czechoslovakia, the enunciation of the Brezhnev Doctrine, and the 1969 clashes between Soviet and Chinese troops on the Ussuri River. Peking, after a serious internal debate which probably was a major factor in Lin Piao's fall from power, decided that Moscow rather than Washington was the principal source of danger.[12] This perception was probably re-inforced by the indications that the United States was gradually—though unevenly, as witness such actions as the invasion of Cambodia in 1970—pulling out of Vietnam. This changing view of the "international environment" made Peking willing and then eager to at least normalize relations with the United States so that it would face only one major enemy and, perhaps, could even be able to use the United States to deter military moves by Moscow. (Peking's need for modern technology, its desire at that time to disrupt U.S.-Japanese relations, and its fear that the world was moving toward at least de facto acceptance of two Chinas also contributed to the shift.)

Peking did not rest all its hopes on improved relations with the United States, but sought to reduce the dangers of Soviet military moves by agreeing at a meeting on September 11, 1969, in Peking between Chou En-lai and Premier Kosygin to open negotiations on border issues. This did not remove China's need for an opening to Washington, but reduced the urgency and allowed Peking more latitude over matters of timing and procedure. It was also probably *one* reason behind the estimated 25 percent reduction in Chinese weapons production between 1971 and 1974, although a political decision to make available fewer resources to the military lest they assume too important a role in the wake of the Cultural Revolution was probably also involved.[13]

On America's part, the Nixon Doctrine was the first attempt to formulate a new policy. Presented at a news conference on Guam in 1969, it was vague and imprecise. The Administration never satisfactorily clarified the confusion surrounding it—perhaps partly because it was still unsure of its own course and partly because it regarded ambiguity as politically and diplomatically necessary if it was to gain the flexibility it sought. In any case, it was interpreted by some as a movement toward neo-isolationism and by others as a return to a more cautious containment stance, but its gaps and inconsistencies indicated that it represented more of a stop-gap response to domestic political pressures to reduce foreign policy burdens than a carefully calculated and integrated policy. Moreover, by early 1972 the Administration had shifted to speaking of world politics in balance-of-power terms.

A reduced American effort in Asia would become possible if (1) the United States were willing to accept losses in what was still seen as a struggle with the Communist powers, which was unacceptable to the Nixon Administration; (2) if its allies would and could do more for their own defense, which was possible for some of them but not for the most hard-pressed; (3) if the United States were to return to some version of the strategy of massive retaliation, which would hardly be appropriate in the strategic environment of the 1970s; or (4) if the magnitude of the "threat" posed by the Communist countries were less—or could be made less—than it had previously appeared. The fourth offered a way out in two respects. First, there was a growing American appreciation that the forces of nationalism in the Third World limited the potential for Soviet or Chinese (as well as American) influence. The fall of men such as Nkrumah, Ben Bella, and Sukarno demonstrated that hard-won positions could quickly vanish. The second and more important realization, however, was that the Sino-Soviet quarrel had reached such intensity that the United States could, if it played its hand skillfully, benefit from it—although not if it led to full-scale war.

A cautious series of probes was undertaken by the United States. U.S. public statements toward China became more conciliatory, and travel and trade restrictions were relaxed. Diplomatic probes were made through third parties such as Pakistan, which had good relations with both China and the United States. The path was an uneven one, however, especially because of internal Chinese resistance to the new policy proposed by Mao and Chou. Their opponents apparently argued that the continuing American involvement in the Vietnam war made a détente with the United States undesirable. The U.S military move into Cambodia in 1970 set back the process of accommodation. But when the United States did not intervene to support the South Vietnamese troops that moved into Laos early in 1971, the dominant view in Peking accepted the Nixon Administration's seriousness about disengaging from Vietnam.

Shortly thereafter, Peking extended an invitation to an American table tennis team to make what amounted to a "semi-official" visit to China—a clear sign that progress was being made. Nonetheless, few people anywhere were prepared for the dramatic news on July 15, 1971, that Henry Kissinger had secretly visited Peking for talks with Chou En-lai, or for the July 16 announcement in the *People's Daily* that President Nixon had been invited to visit China.

The United States faced four major tasks at this point in its policy regarding China: (1) it had to reassure its Asian allies, who had been badly shaken by the sharp change in U.S. policy and by the fact that they had not been consulted or even adequately informed before the public announcement; (2) it needed to sustain the momentum toward better relations; (3) it needed to move toward institutionalizing the new relationship to the extent possible; and (4) it had to work out, partly through trial and error, the substance of its policy and its implications for American foreign policy generally. Each task, presenting different problems, has been performed with varying degrees of success.

The United States has been reasonably successful in dealing with the impact of its new China policy upon its allies. Relations with Japan were seriously strained during 1971 and

1972 (by economic disputes as well as the China issue), but gradually the two countries worked out their problems. By 1974-75 Japanese-American relations were free of major problems in the judgment of knowledgeable private observers as well as officials of the two governments.[14] The picture was more complex regarding America's smaller allies, especially the Republic of China, but continued U.S. assurances of support—and the fact that such assurances were honored— gradually convinced these allies that despite their more difficult positions they were not simply being abandoned to their fate. (Strains in the relations between the United States and the Republic of Korea in the early 1970s were due as much to American concern over domestic political trends in South Korea as to Seoul's concern over America's new China policy.) The Vietnam debacle in 1975, and the Administration's reaction to it, may in the short run have damaged the confidence of certain Asian countries, such as Thailand and the Philippines, as much as the shift in China policy.

The necessary momentum in Sino-American relations was maintained from 1971 until late 1973 or early 1974. Kissinger's visits in October 1971 and U.S. willingness to see Peking become a member of the United Nations were sufficient, despite U.S. opposition to the expulsion of Taipei, to set the stage for the Nixon visit in February 1972. The Shanghai Communiqué issued on February 27, 1972, revealed a considerable amount about the policies of the two governments, although it naturally left much unsaid. It contained: (1) a brief factual account of Nixon's visit; (2) separate statements by the two sides of their respective views on international relations, on Indochina, Korea, Japan, and South Asia; (3) an agreement on general principles of international relations followed by the statement of four principles of conduct specifically relating to the United States and China, including the anti-hegemony principle; (4) separate statements by both sides on Taiwan; (5) agreement by both sides on specific steps to further "broaden the understanding between the two peoples."[15] While some disagreements were ignored, others were set forth openly in an attempt to give the document credibility.

There was also progress toward a more institutionalized relationship when, during Kissinger's February 1973 visit to Peking, the two governments agreed that China and the United States were to establish liaison offices in each other's capitals. This was an unprecendented step, for these were de facto diplomatic missions to be headed by distinguised diplomats. Peking's willingness to do this was an important concession in view of its repeated assertions that it would not send its officials to Washington as long as the Republic of China embassy was there. Trade also grew rapidly—from $4.9 million (in both directions) in 1971 to $803.6 million in 1973, and visits by various officials, special delegations, and others expanded the scope of the relationship.

Since early 1974 there has been a stalemate. Many events have cast their shadows over the relationship. These include President Nixon's preoccupation with Watergate, the appointment of a senior diplomat as the new U.S. Ambassador to the Republic of China, the opening of two new ROC consulates in the United States, the decline in trade in 1975 and 1976 as China's need for grain imports decreased, President Ford's reluctance to loosen ties with Taiwan after the 1975 Vietnam debacle, and occasional frictions in the cultural exchange program.[16] Peking's greatest concern, however, was that the United States was not vigorous enough in its opposition to the expansion of Soviet influence and was deceiving itself about the possibility of détente with the U.S.S.R.[17] Peking was particularly worried by the Vladivostok Accord of November

1974, the Helsinki Agreement of August 1975, and the dismissal of Secretary of Defense James Schlesinger in November 1975, although the increase in the U.S. military budget passed by Congress in 1976 seemed to ease China's fears.[18] The periodic reduction of U.S. forces on Taiwan and President Ford's visit to Peking in December 1975 were enough to prevent serious backsliding, but not enough to ensure continuing progress. Secretary Kissinger, anticipating some significant differences, told the Economic Club of Detroit on the eve of President Ford's visit that

> Disagreements in ideology and national interests exist; there will be no attempt to hide them. It is inevitable, therefore, that each side will determine its own policies according to its own situation and perception of its national interest. These are not subject to the instruction of the other. Both of us are self-reliant; both of us understand the difference between rhetoric and action, between tactics and basic strategy.[19]

The fact that the types of world the two countries want to see develop bear little resemblance to each other was soon spelled out. Teng Hsiao-ping's December 1975 toast to President Ford, the leader of a country which has placed a high value on stability in the world, illustrates this in graphic terms. After speaking of the normalization process, Teng went on to say that

> At present, a more important question confronts the Chinese and American peoples—that of the international situation. Our basic view is: There is great disorder under heaven and the situation is excellent. The basic contradictions in the world are sharpening daily. The factors for

both revolution and war are clearly increasing. Countries want independence, nations want liberation, and the people want revolution—this torrential tide of our time is mounting. In particular, the third world has emerged and grown in strength, and has become a force that is playing an important role in the international arena, a force that must not be neglected. On the other hand, the contention for world hegemony is intensifying and, strategically, Europe is the focus of this contention. Such continued contention is bound to lead to a new world war. This is independent of man's will. Today it is the country which most zealously preaches peace that is the most dangerous source of war. Rhetoric about "détente" cannot cover up the stark reality of the growing danger of war.[20]

These phrases (except for the idea that man's will cannot control events) have a Maoist ring to them, and the fact that they were featured in many Chinese pronouncements suggested continued deference to Mao's personal outlook. But that does not tell us whether they are largely rhetoric or an accurate reflection of the views, aspirations and policies of other Chinese leaders—or a mixture of these factors. Whatever the answer, it raises some basic questions about the interests the two countries have in common. Finally, the deaths of Chou and Mao in 1976 and the ensuing leadership struggle added new complications to a delicate situation.

Yet if the differences and difficulties loom large as of early 1977—and there should be no attempt to minimize them—the Sino-American détente has two very important achievements to its credit. It has reduced the dangers of any Sino-American war, and it provided enough flexibility and resilience to the East Asian scene so that the Communist victories in Vietnam, Laos and Cambodia did not fundamentally alter the Asian balance of power.[21] Whatever its future, these are substantial accomplishments.

AMERICAN INTERESTS AND INFLUENCE

One of the most striking aspects of Sino-American relations is the limited *direct* importance that United States bilateral interests in China are likely to assume in the world's most populous country during the next five to ten years.[22] Alexander Eckstein and Lucian Pye point out in their chapters both the potentials and the problems involved in economic and cultural relations, and so only a few sentences are appropriate here. In 1975, U.S. trade with China amounted to approximately 10 percent of our trade with Taiwan or South Korea, and less than 3 percent of our trade with Japan.[23] Chinese exports to the United States have steadily increased, and China had a trade surplus in 1976, which somewhat expands the potential scope and volume of Sino-American trade. Yet if one accepts quite optimistic forecasts about the potential growth of Sino-American trade, it is unlikely to rise much above 1 percent of total U.S. trade in the early 1980s. We can be confident that there will be no U.S. capital investments in China, although there may be some private or official loans. Tourism will remain extremely limited. Technology transfers from the United States to China may grow if Peking continues its present economic policy, but they are likely to be of more importance to China than to the United States. Other cultural contacts and exchanges will be valuable in increasing the knowledge—and probably the understanding—each society has about the other, but they are likely to remain modest in size and scope. Chinese leaders remain fearful that their society will be contaminated by alien influences, and will rigorously control contacts with other societies. Yet it would be a mistake to downplay the value of economic and cultural relations, for their *absence* would be a sign of deteriorating political relations and would indicate that China and the United States were unable to cooperate in dealing with certain very important multilateral issues.

But if our bilateral interests are significant but of limited direct scope at present, what is the nature and importance of China for American foreign policy? One can set forth several general propositions on this subject. The United States has extremely important interests—strategic and economic—in East Asia. Our trade with this area is about as large as our trade with the European Community. We do not want any single power to dominate in the area, for such domination would threaten America's entire position in the Western Pacific. Thus we want, as Ralph Clough has phrased it, "to consolidate a stable four-power equilibrium in East Asia and reduce the risk of big-power war." [24] Our main interest in a sound relationship with China lies chiefly in the contribution that it can make toward the realization of our broader goals in East Asia and the world, and this makes our relations with China a matter of great though not vital importance. There are dilemmas involved, however, for a weak and divided China would be a tempting target for manipulation and intervention, but an increasingly strong China will have greater capabilities to influence—or even dominate—many of the nations around it.

Difficulties also arise when one attempts to define the nature of the multipolar balance that would be most beneficial to us. Sino-Soviet hostility increases American—and Japanese—freedom of maneuver and gives us some leverage with both Moscow and Peking. (The amount of such leverage is widely debated, but it is hard to believe that it is nonexistent.) At the same time, Sino-Soviet hostility makes it virtually impossible to arrange any but the most informal, ad hoc, four-power cooperation in dealing with potential trouble spots such as the Korean peninsula. Similarly, it is difficult to balance our interest in using our relationship with Peking in order to strengthen our hand in negotiations with Moscow with our interest in maintaining our alliance relationships in Asia and in eventually securing the cooperation of China in dealing with global issues such as arms control, the law of the seas, etc.

These interests and issues are matters of great importance to the United States, but our ability to influence the course of events in East Asia varies greatly. At one end of the spectrum, the United States has considerable ability to influence Japanese-American relations. If these are sound, the United States will also have some influence on the evolution of Japan's relations with the Soviet Union and China.

Historically, many Americans have had—and felt their country had—an interest in the evolution of Chinese society. Many Americans would still like to see China become a more open, democratic society, but the chances of any substantial shift in this direction in the foreseeable future are slim. One need not regard the United States as impotent to recognize that it will have only a marginal impact on the future evolution of Chinese society. Similarly, U.S. ability to influence China's position on global problems—or, to put it another way, to help integrate China into a moderate international order—will be limited. As China takes a more active role in international affairs it will learn from its experience, but it will draw its own conclusions.

The extent of American influence on Chinese foreign policy will be determined more by the health of our own society and our general posture in East Asia and the world at large than by our bilateral relationship with Peking. Despite China's rhetorical opposition to the American presence in

Asia, Peking's interest in a working relationship would decline sharply if the United States were to pull out of the Western Pacific and adopt a mid-Pacific stance. Similarly, if Soviet strength and influence increase throughout the rest of the world while America's position erodes substantially, at least some Chinese leaders will be tempted to seek accommodation with Moscow or press the United States harder on issues in contention—or both. Barring such dramatic shifts in U.S. policy or America's position in the world (or sizable U.S. arms sales to China), U.S. influence on the evolution of Sino-Soviet relations will be modest—except to the extent that America's handling of the Taiwan issue affects relations between Peking and Moscow.

TAIWAN AND THE NORMALIZATION OF SINO-AMERICAN RELATIONS

There is no thoroughly satisfactory solution to the Taiwan issue, for too many conflicting principles and conflicting interests are involved. Whatever course the United States takes will also involve some contradictions or inconsistencies with past policies and actions. For example, the principle of self-determination for the people on Taiwan holds considerable appeal for many Americans, although the United States gave little weight to this principle when the 1947 Taiwanese uprising was bloodily suppressed by Nationalist forces from the mainland. Yet the principle of self-determination for Taiwan conflicts with the traditional American position of support for China's national unity and territorial integrity, and continued active support for Taiwanese independence—at least de jure independence—would be a direct challenge to the powerful force of Chinese nationalism.

There is no neat way to escape these dilemmas in the abstract, or even to be completely neutral. What the United States does will in effect help Peking gain control of Taiwan or help the latter—either temporarily or indefinitely—retain its separate existence. Nor will it be possible to settle the Taiwan issue conclusively in the foreseeable future. What is possible is to handle it in such a way as to reduce it to manageable proportions. Peking has made it clear that it expects a long period to elapse between the termination of U.S.-ROC diplomatic and treaty relations and Taiwan's reabsorption by the mainland. The withdrawal of recognition from the ROC would automatically cause the U.S.-ROC security treaty to lapse, since the United States could hardly have a treaty with a government whose existence it did not recognize diplomatically. However, this need not—and should not—mean the abandonment of Taiwan. As Ralph Clough has pointed out, there are a variety of constraints on Peking's ability to gain control of Taiwan. These constraints, together with the talents and resilience demonstrated by Taiwan in recent years, will provide the latter with considerable scope for shaping its own future. Peking's long-term policy is hard to predict. China eventually accepted the separation of Outer Mongolia—although this was done by a weak Nationalist regime and simply accepted by the Communist leaders when they won power—and may in time do the same regarding Taiwan.

In the absence of a substantial increase in Soviet hostility and belligerence toward China, Sino-American relations are likely to remain stalemated until the normalization process referred to in the Shanghai Communiqué is carried to its logical conclusion by shifting diplomatic recognition from the Republic of China to the People's Republic of China. There are several reasons why the United States should make this shift, but only after certain important arrangements regarding

[223]

Taiwan, which are briefly outlined below, have been made. The *first*, already alluded to, is simply that the United States implicitly pledged itself to do so within a reasonable period when it agreed to the Shanghai Communiqué. Credibility has many aspects, and one is involved here. The Carter Administration has announced that it will continue to work for the normalization of relations, although this is not its top international priority.

The *second* point is that the United States has business to conduct with China, which involves both bilateral issues such as trade and multilateral issues such as the law of the sea and, in time, arms control. It is not impossible to deal with such matters under the present arrangements, but the failure to upgrade the liaison offices to embassies highlights the uncertainties surrounding the relationship and thus indicates that it has a certain fragility. The existence of normal diplomatic relations would make the task somewhat easier, although we should not expect any major shifts in China's positions on contentious issues to result from U.S. recognition. Indeed, Peking might for a time adopt a harsher line—or at least a harsher *tone*—on some issues to prove that it was not losing its revolutionary fervor.

The *third* reason, and perhaps the most important one, is the possible cost of failing to establish diplomatic relations with Peking. While, as Akira Iriye points out in Chapter 2, Peking's view of the international environment is more important in determining Chinese foreign policy than winning diplomatic recognition from the United States—or even gaining control of Taiwan, which is quite another matter—a U.S. failure to establish normal diplomatic relations could lead some Chinese leaders to conclude that they would do well to work for better relations with Moscow. One can argue that a Sino-Soviet détente might be beneficial to the United States, but *not* if it came about as an anti-American move before we had normalized relations with China. One of the dangers of the succession struggle in Peking is that policy toward the United States may become caught up in domestic political disputes.

The *fourth* and related reason is that whatever leverage our links with China have given us in dealing with the Soviet Union would be likely to increase—it certainly would not decrease—with the establishment of diplomatic ties. How much leverage U.S. relations with China gives us in our dealings with Moscow, and how much it would increase, cannot be described with any precision, but it probably is of more than marginal significance. Some observers have argued that none of the agreements Moscow made with the United States represented any sacrifice on the U.S.S.R.'s part.[25] Yet it is doubtful that President Nixon would even have been received in Moscow in 1972 while the United States was bombing North Vietnam if he had not been received in Peking first.

The *fifth* and final point is that the United States is the only major world power that does not recognize the People's Republic of China, a situation which will make the United States look increasingly foolish as time passes. The opening to China demonstrated to other countries that the United States intended to base its policy toward East Asia on facts rather than on illusions. Failure to follow through on the initiatives taken would weaken other nations' confidence in American judgment.

There are, it should be frankly admitted, counterarguments that can be set forth for delay or even for a long-term policy of giving top priority to maintaining relations with the ROC on Taiwan. If credibility is involved in our commitment to "normalization," how is one to interpret Henry Kissinger's comment in his 1972 press conference in Shanghai that the

U.S. security treaty with the Republic of China "will be maintained"?[26] Thus the Shanghai Communiqué puts our credibility at stake in one direction, while ending the Security Treaty with the ROC could damage our credibility with our Asian allies. One can argue that we should wait until we can assess the outcome of the succession struggle in Peking and its effect on Chinese foreign policy before we make a major move. The course of Sino-Soviet relations may be little influenced by what moves the United States makes, but may instead be determined by the national interests of the two countries as perceived by their leaders—although these interests will be seen through the prisms of the leaders' memories, ambitions, and ideological outlooks. Moreover, if Sino-Soviet relations remain hostile, Peking cannot afford to alienate the United States. If there is a basic shift in Sino-Soviet relations and the two countries again join forces against the non-Communist world, the United States will need its present Asian allies to maintain an island-chain defense strategy. Finally the U.S. trade with Taiwan is and will long remain larger than trade with the PRC.[27]

While these arguments cannot be dismissed as having little force, they are less convincing than those which argue for recognizing the PRC. Judgments will vary regarding the appropriate timing for shifting our recognition, but it is difficult to see any hope of establishing a constructive Sino-American relationship over the long term in the absence of formal diplomatic links. And this is of overriding importance.

In shifting recognition from Taipei to Peking, it is important that the United States manage the process in a way that does not dangerously destabilize the East Asian scene. We should be aware that our skill in managing this issue will have a profound effect upon the assessment by Asian nations—especially Japan and China, but also the two Koreas and the

Philippines—of American political skill and maturity. The encouragement that we have given Taiwan over the years must be given due weight, although it does not require that we assume full responsibility for Taiwan's fate by *guaranteeing* the existence of its political independence indefinitely. (We cannot be sure that its political system will prove durable, or that the long-term pull of the idea of one China will not eventually influence Taiwanese behavior.) It does mean providing the people in Taiwan with a major voice as to their future without injecting the United States into the middle of the Peking-Taipei dispute. Similarly, we should allow Taipei to make its own decision about continuing its heavy commitment on the offshore islands. The ROC would do well to reduce its garrison of men there, but if the United States insists on such a course it will be assuming more, rather than less, responsibility for Taiwan's defense.

Both negative and positive considerations argue for continued if declining American involvement with Taiwan, although of a different nature than in the past. A complete and abrupt withdrawal of all U.S. support could create such a domestic political uproar in the United States as to force any administration to become more, rather than less, deeply involved with Taiwan. The naive euphoria about the People's Republic that followed the 1971 moves has greatly diminished, and those who favor maintenance of the status quo in our relations with the ROC have become more organized and outspoken. It could also so shake Taiwan's confidence in its future as to lead it to take such precipitous actions as producing nuclear weapons or declaring its independence from the mainland.[28] Either of these moves would make it much more difficult for Peking to pursue a low-key, cautious policy toward Taiwan, and would increase the dangers that Peking would feel compelled to adopt a more forceful policy. Such

[227]

moves would also be highly disruptive to Sino-American relations as well as to other parts of East Asia, especially Japan and South Korea. China's interests in preventing such drastic moves coincide with those of the United States, and these overlapping interests—at least in the short term—offer reasonable hope that such disruptions can be prevented. Nonetheless, the move will require careful preparation of American public opinion by the Carter Administration so that a shift in diplomatic relations does not appear to involve the abandonment of Taiwan.

The United States can proceed in either—or both—of two ways to assure those on Taiwan that withdrawal of diplomatic ties does not mean an abandonment of U.S. interest in their future. The first is to try to secure from Peking guarantees that it will use only peaceful means to acquire control of Taiwan. This approach is worth trying, but there are two arguments against *relying* on this course.[29] Peking, for quite understandable reasons, refuses to give any explicit assurance that it will renounce the use of force in dealing with what it regards as a Chinese province. Moreover, even if Peking were to give such assurances they would carry very little weight with ROC leaders, whose belief in Peking's good faith is nil. This could change over a generation or two if Peking's actions accorded with its words, but that would provide little help to the United States in dealing with a problem that requires action in the near future. Finally, with a domestic political struggle underway in China, few contenders for leadership are likely to be willing to appear "soft" on the Taiwan issue lest they become vulnerable to the charge that they lack nationalist zeal. A negotiated arrangement might have been possible in 1973 or even 1974 when Chou En-lai was still exercising power, but that opportunity probably was lost with the advent of Watergate.

[228]

The second approach is for the United States unilaterally to take the steps necessary to give Taiwan reasonable confidence in its future. This is not the place to go into this subject in detail, but it is clear that it involves three matters. The *first* point is that Chiang Ching-kuo should be informed of our plans to shift recognition far enough in advance so that he can inform his close associates and supporters in a way that makes clear that we intend to consult with him even as the nature of our relationship changes. This should be coupled with a firm though private warning that if the Republic of China tries to *disrupt* our moves it may lose rather than gain support from the U.S. government. *Second*, we should make the changes in U.S. laws that are necessary to enable Taiwanese-American economic relations to continue largely as before. Peking may object to these measures, for it is sensitive to any *formal* actions taken by the United States regarding continuing involvement with Taiwan. For example, many American business firms which have joined the U.S.-Republic of China Economic Council (established in December 1976) have encountered strong PRC criticism and greater difficulties in doing business with Peking.[30] Nonetheless, China has spoken favorably of the United States following the "Japanese formula," so these changes are unlikely to be unduly provocative to Peking.

The *third* and potentially most difficult issue concerns U.S. moves affecting Taiwan's military security. We should be willing to sell defensive arms and spare parts to Taiwan, not hinder the Taiwanese from setting up their own arms industries, and encourage them to diversify their sources of supply as much as is feasible. Such moves should be played in a low key, and Peking probably should be told in advance that we plan to follow this course. (Since Administration officials will have to set forth their policy on this issue to congressional committees it can hardly be kept secret.) Peking probably will object, but not so strongly as to refuse to establish diplomatic relations with the United States under these circumstances. We should not attempt to replace the security treaty with an explicit unilateral commitment to protect Taiwan. A statement that we would look upon any major use of force in East Asia as a cause for reassessing our own policy and strategy would cushion the shock Taiwan will experience when the treaty lapses. Finally, we should make it clear that any arrangement the two governments work out between themselves to settle the issue peacefully will be acceptable to us.

AMERICAN POLICIES AFTER NORMALIZATION

After recognizing Peking the United States will still face complex choices in its policies toward China, especially as they relate to American policy toward the Soviet Union and toward the East Asian region. The difficulties will be increased by the fact that Chinese domestic politics, about which we know little (except by hindsight), will influence Chinese foreign policy. We know there are "radical" and "moderate" forces and issues, but the positions of individual Chinese officials sometimes shift. The "moderates" apparently favor greater Chinese involvement in international affairs (and some may want to improve relations with Moscow as well as Washington), while the "radicals" generally seem to prefer a more inward-looking China which places greater emphasis on self-reliance. Similarly, American domestic politics will from time to time create pressures on our policies toward China. Given the secrecy of Chinese politics and the complexity and unpredictability of both Chinese and American politics, the potential for misunderstanding and for mistakes is great. There is no way to

[230]

eliminate these dangers, but American leaders can reduce them somewhat by being as candid and consistent as possible over the years.

The issues facing the United States will include the extent to which it should pursue an even-handed policy toward China and the Soviet Union, as distinct from supporting one against the other; the extent to which it should insist upon reciprocity (or quid pro quos) from Peking, especially regarding issues in contention; the desirability and feasibility of encouraging a Sino-Soviet détente; the appropriate U.S. response in the event of a Sino-Soviet détente which occurs without any U.S. involvement; and the importance of Japan, and U.S. relations with it, on the East Asia scene.

To discuss the last item first, we should recognize that America's ability to deal successfully with both Moscow and Peking (whatever the state of their bilateral relations) will be enhanced by a sound U.S.-Japanese relationship. Japan has taken advantage of the Sino-Soviet dispute and the American opening to China to expand its relations with both mainland neighbors without undermining its links with the United States. Tokyo's ability to follow this course is enhanced by its defense ties with the United States. Japan would like to maintain a certain balance in its relations with Peking and Moscow, but the latter has been both rigid and inept in its dealings with Tokyo. Thus Japan's links with China are likely to be closer than its relations with the U.S.S.R. because of greater cultural affinities, geographic proximity, and widespread Japanese fear and distrust of the Soviet Union. At the same time, the contrasting responses of Japan and China to the impact of the West have made them very different societies, and their conflicting interests and policies on certain important points create elements of rivalry between them. In any case, Japan does not want to move dramatically or irreversibly closer to Peking than to Moscow. Unless the latter reacts to Japan's "tilt" toward China with unmitigated hostility, Tokyo will try to lean first in one direction and then in another, attempting to use whatever links it forges with Peking as leverage on Moscow, and vice versa. Thus there is at present considerable harmony between Japanese and American policies toward China and the Soviet Union.[31]

Next, what should be the guidelines and priorities for U.S. policy toward China as it relates to American policy toward the U.S.S.R.? This requires consideration of the likely trend in Sino-Soviet affairs, a complex and uncertain matter which can only be touched upon briefly in this essay. Basically, however, both an open military conflict and a renewal of the former type of Sino-Soviet alliance are extremely unlikely. The former would be a disaster for both countries and probably for the world, and the strife, acrimony and distrust that have developed over the past fifteen years virtually rule out the latter. Moscow has tried to normalize relations on a bilateral and state-to-state basis for the past several years—and especially since the death of Mao—but has had little response from Peking, while both continue to struggle in the arena of world politics and over ideological issues.[32] Moreover, the major Soviet military buildup in Asia since 1969 and Moscow's determination to be an Asian and a Pacific power have created an entirely new military problem for the Chinese, which will remain a source of serious concern. Over the next few years relations are likely to range from a continuation of the present level of hostility to a Sino-Soviet détente (with a longer-term possibility of a rapprochement involving very limited cooperation), although the possibility of a Sino-Soviet détente has increased somewhat since Mao has passed from the scene. Specialists on Sino-Soviet affairs differ in their judgments on the most likely development within this range of possibilities.[33] I can only conclude that the United States should be prepared for either eventuality in view of the many unexpected developments that have occurred over the past three decades in East Asia.

In the event of continued Sino-Soviet hostility, one can argue that since the Soviet Union is our major challenger in the world the United States should actively support China against the U.S.S.R.[34] Without elaborating details, such support could range from granting China (but not the Soviet Union) preferential trade status and cooperating diplomatically with Peking against Moscow in other parts of Asia and Africa, through the sale of military-related technology and weapons themselves, and finally to supporting China's position in the Sino-Soviet border dispute. Among these issues the crucial ones are likely to be those involving military technology and arms sales. Trade preferences and some diplomatic cooperation are unlikely to make any basic change in the character of the triangular relationship of China, the U.S.S.R., and the United States, and Peking probably does not expect (and may not even want) U.S. support in its border dispute.

Under what circumstances would a policy of actively supporting Peking against Moscow be necessary or wise? One can argue that Moscow would react by becoming more accommodating to the United States in an effort to keep Sino-American ties from becoming stronger than those between Moscow and Washington. A more likely Soviet reaction, however, would be to see our actions as inciting rather than merely supporting China, and to adopt a more assertive stance throughout the world. This would intensify Sino-Soviet and Soviet-American rivalries and reduce the chances for further arms control agreements, or for cooperation in such potential trouble spots as Korea. Since our relationship with the Soviets is more important than our relationship with China, this would

[233]

be a high-risk policy. It could also enhance the position of those in Moscow who are more inclined to press China militarily, on the border, thereby increasing the danger of war.

It is also difficult to see any substantial gains that the United States would make from such a policy, which would seriously damage our relations with our Asian allies. While we want China to be strong enough to provide a check on the U.S.S.R., the latter is already in a relatively weak position in East Asia. Its powerful military forces along the Chinese frontier can only be used at a heavy political cost, although the growing strength of the Soviet Pacific fleet is a cause for concern. Its position in Southeast Asia is also weak except in Vietnam and Laos, and even Hanoi does not want to line up completely with Moscow. Sino-American cooperation in South Asia would solidify rather than weaken India's ties to the Soviet Union.[35] And China's power and influence in the Middle East, Africa, and Latin America are extremely limited. China's invitation to James Schlesinger and Drew Middleton—who spoke openly on their returns about China's obsolescent forces—has led some observers to speculate that Peking was preparing the way for a request for American arms support.[36] However, it is doubtful that China would want to become heavily dependent on the United States for arms—or that it would think the United States (especially given what it sees as congressional unpredictability) a reliable supplier.[37]

This suggests that, so long as there are no Soviet moves which bring about a complete collapse of the Soviet-American détente, the best course to follow would be to pursue a general policy of even-handedness. This does not mean identical treatment for the U.S.S.R. and China on every issue. Reality is much too complex for this; the intense suspicions of each side will lead it to see us working more closely with the other than the facts would warrant. Such a rigid interpretation of a policy of even-handedness or equidistance would, in fact, force the United States to respond to Soviet and Chinese moves in a mechanical fashion, in order to maintain equidistance. We should be prepared to lean first to one side and then to the other as circumstances warrant, but the specific issues and problems in our bilateral relations should be examined in the light of our attempt to pursue a balanced policy. In view of Peking's intense desire for self-reliance, its reluctance to seek long-term loans abroad, to give assurances concerning the non-military use of advanced technological equipment, and to permit inspection of such equipment by American officials within China (all matters about which Moscow is more flexible) a rigid even-handedness on our part could benefit the Soviet Union more than China. Since these differences are of Chinese making, there is little the United States can do to influence them in the short run, although the October 1976 sale of two Cyber 172 computers (which have military as well as civilian uses) indicates there is scope for flexibility. A presidential grant of most-favored-nation treatment for Chinese exports to the United States as soon as this is possible and a willingness to have our European allies sell Peking some military-related technology—such as the sale of the Rolls Royce Spey engine—would represent one way to maintain a rough balance. In any case, U.S. recognition of Peking probably would provide adequate momentum for Sino-American relations over the following year or two.

The question of whether, or to what extent, the United States should insist upon reciprocity in Sino-American relations involves three separate matters. The *first* is the proper way to respond to the continuing and generally harsh Chinese rhetoric denouncing America as an imperialist state and a capitalist exploiter. We should not totally ignore such rhetoric (which, while not the same as policy, is not completely

[235]

divorced from it) nor answer in kind—which would be allowing Peking's words to govern our own. American leaders should continue to speak frankly from time to time not only about our hope to improve relations but also about the differences between the two societies and their foreign policies where they conflict. China's rhetoric is addressed more to some audiences (domestic, international Communist, and third world) than to others—and is to a degree a necessary adjunct to a policy of working with the United States. Thus it makes little sense for us to adopt their style simply to insure reciprocity.

The *second* is the question of a rough measure of reciprocity in bilateral relations—economic and cultural affairs—which is a feasible goal to pursue. However, this is a complicated matter to measure and to attain between two such different countries, and we should keep in mind that it works both ways. China may have felt that the U.S. trade surplus until 1976 made this aspect of the relationship of more value to America than to China, especially since most of the technology is available elsewhere.

The *third* aspect is the most complex one, involving as it does conflicting American and Chinese policies over certain important issues in Asia. These are at present not too numerous, since Peking appears to want the United States to remain in Japan and the Philippines—at least for the time being. Korea is another matter, and during 1975 and 1976 Chinese policy became more rigid in its opposition to South Korea as an "illegitimate" state and more outspoken in its support of North Korea. American and Chinese interests—as perceived by the two governments—overlap chiefly in that neither wants a war on the Korean peninsula, for it would imperil the Sino-American détente and the general peace in East Asia. As long as Peking remains intransigent on the issue of South Korea's basic right to exist, the United States can have little hope for reducing tensions on the Korean peninsula, and we must be prepared to oppose China on most aspects of the Korean issue.

With the United States reducing its involvement in South and Southeast Asia, these should not be areas of important Sino-American friction in the next few years unless Peking's support for revolutionary movements expands substantially beyond the rhetorical and nominal stage of recent years. China's problems with the Soviet Union on its northern frontier, combined with Peking's uneasy relations with Hanoi, are likely to result in a relatively cautious Chinese policy in Southeast Asia as long as no other major power appears to be gaining predominant influence there. The Soviet Union is unlikely to be able to expand its influence substantially, and Peking appears less concerned in 1976 than it was five years earlier that Japanese political and military power would follow in the wake of its expanding economic role.[38]

More difficult issues may arise over conflicting claims in the East and South China Seas, where U.S. allies and American oil companies have interests. Since January 1974, China has seized the Paracels (then held by South Vietnam, but claimed by Hanoi). Peking has also pressed its claim to the Spratly Islands farther south (claimed by Vietnam and the Philippines) in militant and chauvinistic terms, which has raised serious concerns about Chinese intentions regarding these issues. At the same time, Peking has taken a relatively relaxed position over the Senkaku Islands claimed by Japan and China.[39]

Arguments about encouraging a Sino-Soviet détente require an appraisal of the nature and extent of American influence on relations between Moscow and Peking. This is a complex and controversial subject, and a sense of proportion is essential. On the one hand, there is very little the United States can do to "fine-tune" the relationship between Moscow and Peking. This judgment reflects three separate but related convictions. First, one of the key influences on Sino-Soviet relations will be the domestic policies of the two countries—especially China—which we find difficult to understand, much less influence in any substantial way. Second, U.S. policies that would move the two countries closer together would involve such basic shifts in America's stance in the world—becoming either isolationist or much more interventionist in a way China thought threatened its security—as to carry unacceptable costs at home or in our relations with other nations in the world. Finally, the structure of the U.S. government, with power divided between the Executive and a more assertive Congress, makes it almost impossible to orchestrate a policy that even attempts such a delicate maneuver on a long-term basis.

This is not to say that U.S. actions can have no impact on trends in Sino-Soviet relations. Continued U.S. recognition of the Republic of China, as argued earlier, probably would push China and the U.S.S.R. closer together, and a strong "tilt" toward Peking could exacerbate Sino-Soviet relations. Less dramatically, there is usually a gap in what Moscow and Peking see as the present reality and what they fear might happen between the other and the United States. Peking's fear that a Soviet-American détente was developing in 1969 and 1970 probably increased its desire for an opening to the United States, and the progress in Sino-American relations in 1971-73 probably caused Soviet leaders to take steps to preserve the Soviet-American détente. By leaning first in one direction and then in another we can influence the policies of both toward us—and thus at times influence their relations with each other. But our actions will be only one of the elements influencing their relations, and seldom the most important one.

The inability of Washington to maneuver Moscow and Peking into what some observers regard as the most desirable relationship from the American point of view does not mean that such a development may not result from the moves of the two adversaries themselves. Thus far there is no sign of any Sino-Soviet détente, and the Soviet and Chinese leaders continue to regard their counterparts with fear and scorn. If tensions along the Sino-Soviet border have lessened, the conflict has been pressed in every other arena in which the two countries have the power to act. Yet there may be some men in high positions in Moscow and Peking who recognize that their mutual hostility costs both nations dearly, and that even a limited détente could have important benefits: reduced military costs and dangers, greater trade opportunities, and the reduced ability of the United States to benefit from their differences. Chinese leaders who think in such terms would not *necessarily* want to see Sino-American relations deteriorate if Sino-Soviet relations became less hostile, but would be seeking to reduce the dangers they see China facing from both superpowers. Few if any Chinese leaders trust the U.S.S.R., and concern that an active anti-American policy might in time lead to Soviet-American collusion probably will influence Chinese policy.

Thus if a détente occurs it probably will be a limited one, which will provide both dangers and opportunities for the United States.[40] One danger is that many Americans will read more into any change—such as a Sino-Soviet border settlement—than is warranted, and will feel betrayed by China. This danger will be acute if a détente occurs shortly after we have shifted recognition from Taipei to Peking. The United States can hardly afford to pass through another cycle of euphoria and disillusionment in its attitude toward China. The need to avoid it places a responsibility upon U.S. leaders to explain both the importance of and the limitations upon our relationship with Peking to the American people. Another danger is that China could in time turn toward seeking hegemony over its smaller neighbors. This would hardly be surprising behavior for a major power, but it could create problems for Tokyo and Washington if Peking's goals appeared to be to exclude Japan and America from playing a role in the area. Finally, a substantial improvement in Sino-Soviet relations that was motivated by a mutual desire to cooperate against the United States, while unlikely, would create a basic change in world politics and would represent a move back to Cold War conditions.

The opportunity presented by a Sino-Soviet détente lies in the possibility—and it is no more than that—that if Sino-Soviet relations are not dominated by bitterness and hostility the two countries will not feel the need to compete with each other on so many key issues. This probably would be a slow process, for competition and struggle have become a way of life for both governments. It will be difficult for Moscow to refrain from trying to influence Chinese politics in a pro-Soviet direction. This apparently is just what some Chinese leaders fear most, and such actions could stir Chinese nationalism in new anti-Soviet directions. But if the two countries gradually arrive at a modus vivendi, this will present a long-term possibility of achieving a measure of progress on dealing with the many important regional and global issues that will be on the international agenda in the final decades of this century. The major task of dealing with these issues will fall to the non-Communist industrial nations—both in their relations among themselves and with the developing countries. However, the Soviet Union and China may assume increasing importance in international economic and environmental issues, and may in time conclude that they have a stake in cooperating to create a moderate international order. It is difficult to see a Sino-Soviet détente that makes such cooperation possible as harmful to U.S. interests.

But it would be a major mistake for the United States to think of its policies toward the Soviet Union and China primarily in terms of how its actions will affect their relations with each other. That should be only one aspect of America's policies toward East Asia and world politics generally. Primary attention should be directed toward maintaining a sound relationship with Japan, toward working for a gradual improvement in U.S. bilateral relations with both the Soviet Union and China, and toward trying to find ways to mitigate the disputes between the United States on the one hand and the Soviet Union and China on the other that involve third countries. Our relationships with these two major powers are likely to be more competitive than cooperative for the foreseeable future, but this only increases the need to combine imagination and flexibility with an underlying strength and firmness.

The advantage of no longer having China as a military adversary whose every move must be countered is a considerable gain, and fully justifies the attempt made over the past six years to diminish tensions. Yet Americans should remember that Chinese leaders believe that they have many basic grievances—historical and current—against the United States—and only time can ease these views. There will be setbacks as well as achievements in the relationship, and it will be an uneasy and ambiguous one. The American people can accept these facts, but only if they are presented by their political leaders in a forceful and forthright manner.

Notes

1. Michel Tatu, *The Great Power Triangle: Washington-Moscow-Peking*, The Atlantic Papers No. 3 (Paris: The Atlantic Institute, 1970).

2. For appraisals of the Soviet reaction, see Ian Clark, "Sino-American Relations in Soviet Perspective," *Orbis*, Vol. XVII, No. 2 (Summer 1973), pp. 480-92, and George Ginsburgs, "Moscow's Reaction to Nixon's Jaunt to Peking," in Gene J. Hsiao, ed., *Sino-American Détente and Its Policy Implications* (New York: Praeger, 1974).

3. One prominent dissenter was Nicholas J. Spykman, who argued that a strong China would be in a position to dominate much of Asia, and that the United States should seek to balance China by working with a defeated (but not destroyed) Japan and other Asian countries. Nicholas J. Spykman, *America's Strategy in World Politics* (New York: Harcourt, Brace & Co., 1942), pp. 469-70.

4. A fourth possibility, but a very remote one, was to write off the Chinese Nationalists *and* shift American support to other groups in China, especially the Communists. For an interesting essay on this point, see Barbara Tuchman, "If Mao Had Come to Washington: An Essay in Alternatives," *Foreign Affairs*, Vol. 51, No. 1 (October 1972), pp. 44-64.

5. "On the People's Democratic Dictatorship," *Selected Works of Mao Tse-tung* (Peking: Foreign Language Press, 1961), Vol. IV, p. 417. The key events and documents dealing with United States and Chinese policies toward each other have been compiled and analyzed in Roderick MacFarquhar's, *Sino-American Relations, 1949-71* (New York: Praeger Publishers, for The Royal Institute of International Affairs, 1972).

6. For an excellent short analysis of the complexities of Sino-American relations and the importance of policy involving one· country in the domestic politics of the other, see Michel Oksenberg and Robert B. Oxnam, *China and America: Past and Future* (New York: Foreign Policy Association, Headline Series No. 235, 1977).

7. For example, the treaty with the Republic of Korea was designed in part to gain Seoul's acquiescence in the armistice agreement worked out between 1951 and 1953. Interestingly, it was Moscow rather than Peking that made the overtures that set the armistice talks in motion even though Chinese troops were the ones directly involved in the fighting.

8. "Report on the Near East," *Department of State Bulletin*, Vol. XXIII (No. 729, June 15, 1953), pp. 831-35.

9. The policy was also largely defensive despite such gestures as the "unleashing" of Chiang Kai-shek in 1953, the encouragement of small-scale Nationalist raids against the mainland in the early and mid-1950s, and covert operations in Tibet in the late 1950s and early 1960s.

10. Yet American and Chinese leaders learned to "manage" their conflicts without direct military clashes after the Korean War. See Jan Kalicki, *The Pattern of Sino-American Crises* (New York: Cambridge University Press, 1975).

11. For a comprehensive appraisal, see Allen Whiting, "The Use of Force in Foreign Policy by the People's Republic of China," *The Annals of the American Academy of Political and Social Science*, Vol. 402 (July 1972), pp. 55-66.

12. The initial probes began in 1968. U.S. Undersecretary of State Nicholas deB. Katzenbach and Senator Mike Mansfield suggested in June 1968 that the trade embargo be relaxed, and in November the

Chinese Ministry of Foreign Affairs proposed that Peking and Washington conclude "an agreement on the Five Principles of Peaceful Coexistence." *Peking Review*, No. 48 (November 29, 1968). However, Peking abruptly cancelled the first ambassadorial talks scheduled in two years within a month of the inauguration of the Nixon Administration, suggesting uncertainty and divisions within the Chinese leadership.

13. Sydney Jammes, "The Chinese Defense Burden, 1965-1974," in *China: A Reassessment of the Economy*, Joint Economic Committee of the Congress of the United States, July 10, 1975, p. 463.

14. Philip H. Trezise, "The Second Phase in U.S.-Japan Relations," *Pacific Community*, Vol. 6, No. 3 (April 1975), pp. 340-51. These views were expressed before the Lockheed scandal became a political issue.

15. For an examination of Chinese use of the anti-hegemony principle, see Joachim Glaubitz, "Anti-Hegemony Formulas in Chinese Foreign Policy," *Asian Survey*, Vol. XVI, No. 3 (March 1976), pp. 205-15.

16. Peking, for example, accused the United States of "undisguised interference in China's internal affairs and a flagrant violation of the principles of the Shanghai Communique" by refusing to ban certain activities by Tibetan exiles. *Peking Review*, No. 42 (October 10, 1975).

17. Despite Chinese complaints about the U.S. failure to counter the Soviets vigorously, their propaganda still presented the United States as the world's strongest nation—and one resolved to stand up to Moscow—in mid-1975. Foreign Broadcast Information Service (FBIS), *Trends in Communist Propaganda*, Vol. XXVI, No. 25 (June 25, 1975) and No. 30 (July 30, 1975). Early in 1974 Peking also publicized favorably the increases in U.S. defense spending made in reaction to the Soviet defense buildup. FBIS (People's Republic of China) January 24, 1977.

18. FBIS, *Trends in Communist Propaganda*, Vol. XXVI, No. 45 (November 12, 1975). FBIS (PRC), May 10, 1976.

19. Bureau of Public Services, Department of State, November 24, 1975.

20. *Peking Review*, No. 49 (December 5, 1975), p. 8.

21. Some observers have also concluded that Peking as well as Moscow contributed to the 1972 Vietnam cease-fire agreement. See Tad Szulc, "Behind the Vietnam Cease-Fire Agreement," *Foreign Policy*, No. 15 (Summer 1974), especially pp. 36-45; and Michel Tatu, "Moscow, Peking, and the Conflict in Vietnam" (p. 20), in Anthony Lake, *The Legacy of Vietnam: The War, American Society, and the Future of American Foreign Policy* (New York: New York Univeristy Press, for the Council on Foreign Relations, 1976).

22. For an excellent statement as to the long-term importance of Sino-American bilateral relations, and one that does not ignore the many difficulties in forging stronger links, see Michel Oksenberg, *The United States and China* (New York: Lippincott, 1976).

23. International Monetary Fund, IBRD, *Direction of Trade*, February 1976, pp. 2-4.

24. It should be noted that the nature of each of the four powers is quite different and they possess different kinds of power, which limits the relevance of classical balance-of-power theories. See A. Doak Barnett, "The New Multipolar Balance in East Asia: Implications for United States Policy," *The Annals of the American Academy of Political and Social Sciences*, Vol. 390 (July 1970); and William J. Barnds, "Changing Power Relationships in East Asia," in Hedley Bull, ed., *Asia and the Western Pacific: Towards a New International Order* (Sydney T. Nelson & Sons, 1975), pp. 3-20.

25. See Leslie H. Gelb, "Washington Fears Losing Leverage

Against Moscow," *The New York Times*, November 30, 1975, for an analysis of this issue.

26. *Department of State Bulletin*, March 20, 1972, p. 428.

27. For a well-argued view that the United States policy should work to assure that Taiwan remains an independent nation, see Robert A. Scalapino, *Asia and the Road Ahead* (Berkeley: University of California Press, 1975), pp. 234-41.

28. The possibility of Taiwan turning to the U.S.S.R., and the latter responding positively, is slight unless Moscow had concluded that there was no chance of improving Sino-Soviet relations for the indefinite future.

29. Ralph Clough, who discusses Taiwan in much more detail in Chapter 5, believes that the chances of negotiating reciprocal concessions are sufficiently good to make a major diplomatic effort to do so.

30. *The Wall Street Journal*, January 25, 1977.

31. For a more extensive discussion of this subject, see William J. Barnds, "Japan and Its Mainland Neighbors: An End to Equidistance?" *International Affairs*, Vol. 52, No. 1 (January 1976), pp. 27-38.

32. See Kenneth G. Lieberthal, "Sino-Soviet Relations: Moscow's View," *Problems of Communism*, July-August 1976, pp. 82-84; and "1976 in Retrospect: Soviet Détente Fraud Exposed," *Peking Review*, January 14, 1977, pp. 31-32.

33. For a view that China will continue to represent a major political threat in the minds of Soviet leaders, see Robert C. Horn, "Sino-Soviet Relations in an Era of Détente," *Asian Affairs*, May-

June 1976, pp. 287-304. For a view that a Sino-Soviet détente is likely after Mao's departure, see Donald S. Zagoria, "Mao's Role in the Sino-Soviet Conflict," *Pacific Affairs*, Vol. 47, No. 2 (Summer 1974), pp. 139-53.

34. The idea of *favoring* Moscow over Peking has rightly had few American supporters, even among those arguing for U.S.-Soviet détente, although Soviet officials apparently broached the idea of a measure of "collusion" between the two superpowers to their American counterparts during the SALT negotiations. See John Newhouse, *Cold Dawn: The Story of SALT* (New York: Holt, Rinehart and Winston, 1973), p. 189.

35. India and China took some modest steps toward improved relations in mid-1976, including the exchange of ambassadors for the first time since 1961, but shortly thereafter China reiterated its support for Pakistan's policy of self-determination for the people of Kashmir. FBIS (PRC), June 1, 1976. The Indian government elected in March 1977 announced it would seek a more balanced position between Moscow and Washington, and U.S. policy should be designed to further rather than frustrate this desire.

36. "Inside China Now," *United States News and World Report*, October 18, 1976; *The New York Times*, December 1, 1976; *The Guardian Weekly*, December 26, 1976.

37. For a different view of the appropriate U.S. policy, see Michael Pillsbury, "U.S.-Chinese Military Ties?" *Foreign Policy*, No. 20 (Fall 1975), pp. 50-64; and A. Doak Barnett, "Military-Security Relations between China and the United States," *Foreign Affairs*, Vol. 55, No. 3 (April 1977), pp. 584-97.

38. China restrained its criticism of the United States after the 1975 Communist victory in Vietnam. FBIS, *Trends in Communist Propaganda*, Vol. XXVI, No. 21 (May 29, 1975). Peking also had

good words to say about the efforts of the Association of Southeast Asian (ASEAN) countries to increase their economic cooperation. *Peking Review*, Vol. 18, No. 25, pp. 19, 23.

39. The territories claimed by Peking are also claimed by the Republic of China on Taiwan, which further complicates matters.

40. Many China specialists in the Soviet Union have, since about 1975, become more optimistic about the possibility of a détente within the next five years. It will be interesting to observe whether this optimism persists if the death of Mao does not result in a less hostile Chinese policy.

Index